Preach Liberty:
Selections from the
Bible for Progressives

Edited by
Steve Bachmann

Four Walls Eight Windows, New York

Copyright © 1989 Stephen Bachmann
Illustrations copyright © 1989 John Bowdren

First edition published by:
Four Walls Eight Windows
PO Box 548
Village Station
New York, N.Y. 10014

First printing January 1990.

Library of Congress Cataloging-in-Publication Data:

Bible. English, Authorized. Selections. 1989.
Preach liberty: Selections from the Bible for Progressives/edited by Steve
Bachmann.
—1st ed.
p.   cm.
Consists chiefly of quotations from the King James version of the Bible.
1. Social justice—Biblical teaching. I. Bachmann, Steve, 1951–. II. Title.
BS680.J8B53/ 1989   89-35507   261.8—dc20

ISBN: 0-941423-29-8

CONTENTS

261.8
Bib

INTRODUCTION

The purpose of this book is to reclaim the Bible for the people.

For many whose understanding of the Bible is informed by the interpretations of right wing television and radio preachers—self-proclaimed representatives of God—the Bible has become little more than a justification for the mistreatment of children, the subordination of women, and the undermining of prospects for peace between nations or the survival of the planet.

But the Bible is a book of broader scope. While certain portions of it can be cited for the purposes of the Right, it must also be remembered that the Bible arises from an insurgent tradition.

The Old Testament is based on figures of popular rebellion. The invention of the boycott and general strike can be attibuted to Moses. King David began his career as a Hebrew Robin Hood. Also, the prophets who take the stage at the climax of the Old Testament instituted a tradition of confronting power with truth that has extended into our own times with Martin Luther King.

The hero of the New Testament is Jesus. Like Joe Hill in our own century, he was executed by the authorities for political agitation. His follower St. Paul provides a fascinating study of an organizer establishing mutual aid societies for the poor throughout the ancient world.

The list could be extended for a number of pages, but the point is simple. Whether one's Bible includes the Old Testament, the New Testament, and/or the Apocrypha, the message is consistent: respect for social justice is a precondition for being considered a child of God.

In the civil rights song "We Shall Overcome" one refrain is "God is on our side." *Preach Liberty* suggests that this may be true.

1

VALUES

The Bible expresses a number of values. One of the most prominent is that of social justice. Throughout the Old and New Testaments the Biblical writers state God's expectation that people be fair and treat one another with respect. This obligation falls with particular stringency on the rich and powerful. Accompanying their earthly privileges is a heavy responsibility to sustain justice.

For the Lord your God is God of gods, and Lord of lords, a great God, a mighty, and a terrible, which regardeth no persons, nor taketh reward:

He doth execute the judgment of the fatherless and widow, and loveth the stranger, in giving him food and raiment.

Love ye therefore the stranger: for ye were strangers in the land of Egypt.
—*Deuteronomy 10:17–19*

The spirit of the Lord God is upon me; because the Lord hath anointed me to preach good tidings unto the meek; he

hath sent me to bind up the brokenhearted, to proclaim liberty to the captives, and the opening of the prison to them that are bound.
—*Isaiah 61:1*

Thus speaketh the Lord of hosts, saying, Execute true judgment, and show mercy and compassions every man to his brother:

And oppress not the widow, nor the fatherless, the stranger, nor the poor; and let none of you imagine evil against his brother in your heart.
—*Zechariah 7:9–10*

Now we exhort you, brethren, warn them that are unruly, comfort the feebleminded, support the weak, be patient toward all men.

See that none render evil for evil unto any man; but ever follow that which is good, both among yourselves, and to all men.
—*I Thessalonians 5:14–15*

4

EGALITARIANISM

The Bible's opposition to man-made inequalities is conveyed through a number of recurring themes.

Generally, the Bible asserts that true worth derives from moral worth—to which all people may aspire—as opposed to worldly success, which only a minority can enjoy. Indeed, the Bible frequently suggests that wealth and power undercut the capacity for implementing moral decency. Hence the Bible bears solicitude for the poor and working people and reservations concerning the rich.

Also, social pretense is disapproved of throughout the Bible. This is illustrated most concretely by the story of Jesus. God's Son, the Messiah, does not appear on earth in pomp and glory. Rather, he arrives in a stable because his parents cannot get other lodging. His visitation is first announced to shepherds, not to kings. He dies like a common criminal, humiliated by agents of the state.

Finally, the Bible presents us with a number of "celebrations of revaluation." At a number of junctures the Bible praises the overthrow of the rich and powerful and the elevation of the impoverished and humble.

The Bible's solicitude for society's lower classes suggests that one of its early functions was to give hope to oppressed social groups. In this sense it was and still is a book for the poor and the disenfranchised. However, the Bible's various celebrations of revaluation imply that the hope its readers derived from it did not only relate to events in the afterlife. In advocating revolutionary transformation, the Bible intimates power seizure on the part of the downtrodden.

MORAL WORTH

HEAVEN FAVORS THE RIGHTEOUS OVER THE RICH

All my bones shall say, Lord, who is like unto thee, which deliverest the poor from him that is too strong for him, yea, the poor and the needy from him that spoileth him?
—*Psalms 35:10*

I know that the Lord will maintain the cause of the afflicted, and the right of the poor.
—*Psalms 140:12*

And he shall judge the world in righteousness, he shall minister judgment to the people in uprightness.

The Lord will also be a refuge for the oppressed, a refuge in times of trouble.

And they that know thy name will put their trust in thee: for thou, Lord, has not forsaken them that seek thee.

Sing praises to the Lord, which dwelleth in Zion: declare among the people his doings.

When he maketh inquisition for blood, he remembereth them: he forgetteth not the cry of the humble.
—*Psalms 9:8–12*

The wicked have drawn out the sword, and have bent their bow, to cast down the poor and needy, and to slay such as be of upright conversation.

Their sword shall enter into their own heart, and their bows shall be broken.

A little that a righteous man hath is better than the riches of many wicked.
—*Psalms 37:14–16*

RIGHTEOUSNESS IS MORE VALUABLE THAN WEALTH

Better is a little with righteousness, than great revenues without right.
—*Proverbs 16:8*

6

THE POOR, THE RICH, AND GOD

Then Jesus said unto his disciples, Verily I say unto you, That a rich man shall hardly enter into the kingdom of heaven.

And again I say unto you, It is easier for a camel to go through the eye of a needle, than for a rich man to enter into the kingdom of God.

—Matthew 19:23–24

And Jesus sat over against the treasury, and beheld how the people cast money into the treasury: and many that were rich cast in much.

And there came a certain poor widow, and she threw in two mites, which make a farthing.

And he called unto him his disciples, and saith unto them, Verily I say unto you, That this poor widow hath cast more in, than all they which have cast into the treasury:

For all they did cast in of their abundance; but she of her want did cast in all that she had, even all her living.

—Mark 12:41–44

PROBLEMS FOR THE RICH

But they that will be rich fall into temptation and a snare, and into many foolish and hurtful lusts, which drown men in destruction and perdition.

For the love of money is the root of all evil: which while some coveted after, they have erred from the faith, and pierced themselves through with many sorrows.

—I Timothy 6:9–10

NO SOCIAL PRETENSE

GOD INFORMS THE WORKING PEOPLE

Give ye ear, and hear my voice; hearken, and hear my speech.

Doth the plowman plow all day to sow? doth he open and break the clods of his ground?

When he hath made plain the face thereof, doth he not cast abroad the fitches, and scatter the cummin, and cast in the principal wheat and the appointed barley and the rye in their place?

For his God doth instruct him to discretion, and doth teach him.

For the fitches are not threshed with a threshing instrument, neither is a cart wheel turned about upon the cummin; but the fitches are beaten out with a staff, and the cummin with a rod.

Bread corn is bruised; because he will not ever be threshing it, nor break it with the wheel of his cart, nor bruise it with his horsemen.

This also cometh forth from the Lord of hosts, which is wonderful in counsel, and excellent in working.
—*Isaiah 28:23–29*

JESUS' COMMON BIRTH

And all went to be taxed, every one into his own city.

And Joseph also went up from Galilee, out of the city of Nazareth, into Judaea, unto the city of David, which is called Bethlehem, (because he was of the house and lineage of David:)

To be taxed with Mary his espoused wife, being great with child.

And so it was, that, while they were there, the days were accomplished that she should be delivered.

And she brought forth her firstborn son, and wrapped him in swaddling clothes, and laid him in a manger; because there was no room for them in the inn.

And there were in the same country shepherds abiding in the field, keeping watch over their flock by night.

And, lo, the angel of the Lord came upon them, and the

glory of the Lord shone round about them; and they were sore afraid.

And the angel said unto them, Fear not: for, behold, I bring you good tidings of great joy, which shall be to all people.

For unto you is born this day in the city of David a Saviour, which is Christ the Lord.

And this shall be a sign unto you; Ye shall find the babe wrapped in swaddling clothes, lying in a manger.

And suddenly there was with the angel a multitude of the heavenly host praising God, and saying,

Glory to God in the highest, and on earth peace, good will toward men.

And it came to pass, as the angels were gone away from them into heaven, the shepherds said one to another, Let us now go even unto Bethlehem, and see this thing which is come to pass, which the Lord hath made known unto us.

And they came with haste, and found Mary and Joseph, and the babe lying in a manger.

—*Luke 2:3–16*

JESUS' IGNOBLE DEATH

Then Pilate therefore took Jesus, and scourged him.

And the soldiers platted a crown of thorns, and put it on his head, and they put on him a purple robe, and said, Hail, King of the Jews! and they smote him with their hands.

. . .

Then Pilate delivered Jesus to be crucified. And they took Jesus, and led him away.

And he bearing his cross went forth into a place called the place of a skull, which is called in the Hebrew Golgotha: where they crucified him, and two other with him, on either side one, and Jesus in the midst.

—*John 19:1–3, 16–18*

JESUS CONDEMNS THE ELITE

Woe unto you, Pharisees! for ye love the uppermost seats in the synagogues, and greetings in the markets.

—*Luke 11:43*

10

Woe unto you, lawyers! for ye have taken away the key of knowledge: ye entered not in yourselves, and them that were entering in ye hindered.
—*Luke 12:52*

JESUS DEMONSTRATES HUMILITY

Jesus riseth from supper, and laid aside his garments; and took a towel, and girded himself.

After that he poureth water into a basin, and began to wash the disciples' feet, and to wipe them with the towel wherewith he was girded.

Then cometh he to Simon Peter: and Peter saith unto him, Lord, dost thou wash my feet?

Jesus answered, and said unto him, What I do thou knowest not now; but thou shalt know hereafter.

Peter saith unto him, Thou shalt never wash my feet. Jesus answered him, If I wash thee not, thou hast no part with me.

Simon Peter saidth unto him, Lord, not my feet only, but also my hands and my head.

Jesus saith to him, He that is washed needeth not save to wash his feet, but is clean every whit: and ye are clean, but not all.

For he knew who should betray him; therefore said he, Ye are not all clean.

So after he had washed their feet, and had taken his garments, and was set down again, he said unto them, Know ye what I have done to you?

Ye call me Master and Lord: and ye say well; for so I am.

If I then, your Lord and Master, have washed your feet; ye also ought to wash one another's feet.

For I have given you an example, that ye should do as I have done to you.
—*John 13:4–15*

JAMES CONDEMNS SNOBBERY

My brethren, have not the faith of our Lord Jesus Christ, the Lord of glory, with respect of persons.

For if there come unto your assembly a man with a gold ring, in goodly apparel, and there come in also a poor man in vile raiment;

And ye have respect to him that weareth the gay clothing, and say unto him, Sit thou here in a good place; and say to the poor, Stand thou there, or sit here under my footstool: are ye not then partial in yourselves, and are become judges of evil thoughts?

Hearken, my beloved brethren, Hath not God chosen the poor of this world rich in faith, and heirs of the kingdom which he hath promised to them that love him?

But ye have despised the poor. Do not rich men oppress you, and draw you before the judgment seats?

Do they not blaspheme that worthy name by the which ye are called?

If ye fulfil the royal law according to the Scripture, Thou shalt love thy neighbor as thyself, ye do well:

But if ye have respect to persons, ye commit sin, and are convinced of the law as transgressors.

—*James 2:1–9*

REVALUATIONS

BABIES WILL OVERCOME THE MIGHTY

Out of the mouths of babes and sucklings hast thou ordained strength because of thine enemies, that thou mightest still the enemy and the avenger.
—*Psalms 8:2*

THE MISERABLE WILL BE ENLIGHTENED

Is it not yet a very little while, and Lebanon shall be turned into a fruitful field, and the fruitful field shall be esteemed as a forest?

And in that day shall the deaf hear the words of the book, and the eyes of the blind shall see out of obscurity, and out of darkness.

The meek also shall increase their joy in the Lord, and the poor among men shall rejoice in the Holy One of Israel.
—*Isaiah 29:17–19*

KINGS WILL FALL

And thou, profane wicked prince of Israel, whose day is come, when iniquity shall have an end,

Thus saith the Lord God; Remove the diadem, and take off the crown: this shall not be the same: exalt him that is low, and abase him that is high.

I will overturn, overturn, overturn it: and it shall be no more, until he come whose right it is; and I will give it him.
—*Ezekiel 21:25–27*

The same hour was the thing fulfilled upon Nebuchadnezzar: and he was driven from men, and did eat grass as oxen, and his body was wet with the dew of heaven, till his hairs were grown like eagles' feathers, and his nails like birds' claws.
—*Daniel 4:33*

THE RICH WILL FALL

Let the brother of low degree rejoice in that he is exalted:

But the rich, in that he is made low: because as the flower of the grass he shall pass away.

For the sun is no sooner risen with a burning heat, but it withereth the grass, and the flower thereof falleth, and the grace of the fashion of it perisheth: so also shall the rich man fade away in his ways.
—*James 1:9–11*

MIGHTY CITIES WILL FALL

And the kings of the earth, who have committed fornication and lived deliciously with her, shall bewail her, and lament for her, when they shall see the smoke of her burning,

Standing afar off for the fear of her torment, saying, Alas, alas that great city Babylon, that mighty city! for in one hour is thy judgment come.

And the merchants of the earth shall weep and mourn over her, for no man buyeth their merchandise any more:

The merchandise of gold, and silver, and precious stones, and of pearls, and fine linen, and purple, and silk, and scarlet, and all thyine wood, and all manner vessels of ivory, and all manner vessels of most precious wood, and of brass, and iron, and marble.

And cinnamon, and odours, and ointments, and frankincense, and wine, and oil, and fine flour, and wheat, and beasts, and sheep, and horses, and chariots, and slaves, and souls of men.

And the fruits that thy soul lusted after are departed from thee, and all things which were dainty and goodly are departed from thee, and thou shalt find them no more at all.

The merchants of these things, which were made rich by her, shall stand afar off for the fear of her torment, weeping and wailing,

And saying, Alas, alas that great city, that was clothed in fine linen, and purple, and scarlet, and decked with gold, and precious stones, and pearls!

For in one hour so great riches is come to nought. And every shipmaster, and all the company in ships, and sailors, and as many as trade by sea, stood afar off,

And cried when they saw the smoke of her burning, saying, What city is like unto this great city!

And they cast dust on their heads, and cried, weeping and wailing, saying, Alas, alas, that great city, wherein were made rich all that had ships in the sea by reason of her costliness! for in one hour is she made desolate.
—*Revelations 18:9–19*

THE LORD EXALTS THE LOW

And Mary said, My soul doth magnify the Lord,
And my spirit hath rejoiced in God my Saviour.

For he hath regarded the low estate of his handmaiden: for, behold, from henceforth all generations shall call me blessed.

For he that is mighty hath done to me great things; and holy is his name.

And his mercy is on them that fear him from generation to generation.

He hath showed strength with his arm; he hath scattered the proud in the imagination of their hearts.

He hath put down the mighty from their seats, and exalted them of low degree.

He hath filled the hungry with good things; and the rich he hath sent empty away.
—*Luke 1:46–53*

THE LORD EXALTS THE HUMBLE

And whosoever shall exalt himself shall be abased; and he that shall humble himself shall be exalted.
—*Matthew 23:12*

THE LORD EXALTS THE POOR

And Jesus lifted up his eyes on his disciples, and said, Blessed be ye poor: for yours is the kingdom of God.

Blessed are ye that hunger now: for ye shall be filled. Blessed are ye that weep now: for ye shall laugh.

Blessed are ye, when men shall hate you, and when they shall separate you from their company, and shall reproach you, and cast out your name as evil, for the Son of man's sake.

Rejoice ye in that day, and leap for joy: for, behold, your reward is great in heaven: for in the like manner did their fathers unto the prophets.

But woe unto you that are rich! for ye have received your consolation.

Woe unto you that are full! for ye shall hunger. Woe unto you that laugh now! for ye shall mourn and weep.

Woe unto you, when all men shall speak well of you! for so did their fathers to the false prophets.
—*Luke 6:20–26*

PEACE (NONVIOLENCE)

The Biblical injunctions against violence have been revitalized most recently by the remarkable story of Dr. Martin Luther King. Of equal importance, however, are its condemnations of reliance on military power. As the prophet Hosea suggests, those who acquiesce to the course of the military industrial complex invite social disintegration. The prophet Samuel describes the internal oppressions that result from the establishment of a national security state.

IN PRAISE OF THE MEEK

But the meek shall inherit the earth; and shall delight themselves in the abundance of peace.
—*Psalms 37:11*

HOSEA CONDEMNS RELIANCE ON MILITARY POWER

Ye have plowed wickedness, ye have reaped iniquity; ye have eaten the fruit of lies: because thou didst trust in thy way, in the multitude of thy mighty men.

Therefore shall a tumult arise among thy people, and all thy fortresses shall be spoiled, as Shalman spoiled Betharbel in the day of battle: the mother was dashed in pieces upon her children.
—*Hosea 10:13–14*

SAMUEL CONDEMNS THE NATIONAL SECURITY STATE

Then all the elders of Israel gathered themselves together, and came to Samuel unto Ramah,

And said unto him, Behold, thou art old, and thy sons walk not in thy ways: now make us a king to judge us like all the nations.

But the thing displeased Samuel, when they said, Give us a king to judge us. And Samuel prayed unto the Lord.

And the Lord said unto Samuel, Hearken unto the voice of the people in all that they say unto thee: for they have not rejected thee, but they have rejected me, that I should not reign over them.

According to all the works which they have done since the day that I brought them up out of Egypt even unto this day, wherewith they have forsaken me, and served other gods, so do they also unto thee.

Now therefore hearken unto their voice: howbeit yet protest solemnly unto them, and show them the manner of the king that shall reign over them.

And Samuel told all the words of the Lord unto the people that asked of him a king.

And he said, This will be the manner of the king that shall reign over you: He will take your sons, and appoint them for himself, for his chariots, and to be his horsemen; and some shall run before his chariots.

And he will appoint him captains over thousands, and captains over fifties; and will set them to ear his ground, and to reap his harvest, and to make his instruments of war, and instruments of his chariots.

And he will take your daughters to be confectionaries, and to be cooks, and to be bakers.

And he will take your fields, and your vineyards, and your oliveyards, even the best of them, and give them to his servants.

And he will take the tenth of your seed, and of your vineyards, and give to his officers, and to his servants.

And he will take your menservants, and your maidservants, and your goodliest young men, and your asses, and put them to his work.

He will take the tenth of your sheep: and ye shall be his servants.

And ye shall cry out in that day because of your king which ye shall have chosen you; and the Lord will not hear you in that day.

Nevertheless the people refused to obey the voice of Samuel; and they said, Nay; but we will have a king over us;

That we also may be like all the nations; and that our king may judge us, and go out before us, and fight our battles.
—I Samuel 8:4-20

JESUS CONDEMNS RELIANCE ON MILITARY POWER

And, behold, one of them which were with Jesus stretched out his hand, and drew his sword, and struck a servant of the high priest, and smote off his ear.

Then said Jesus unto him, Put up again thy sword into

his place: for all they that take the sword shall perish with
the sword.
—*Matthew 26:51–52*

PEACEMAKERS ARE GOD'S CHILDREN

Blessed are the peacemakers: for they shall be called
the children of God.
—*Matthew 5:9*

LOVE AND FORGIVE

Then came Peter to him, and said, Lord, how oft shall
my brother sin against me, and I forgive him? till seven
times?

Jesus said unto him, I say not unto thee, Until seven
times: but Until seventy times seven.
—*Matthew 18:21–22*

Ye have heard that it hath been said, Thou shalt love thy
neighbor, and hate thine enemy.

But I say unto you, Love your enemies, bless them that
curse you, do good to them that hate you, and pray for them
which despitefully use you, and persecute you.
—*Matthew 5:43–44*

But I say unto you which hear, Love your enemies, do
good to them which hate you,

Bless them that curse you, and pray for them which
despitefully use you.

And unto him that smiteth thee on the one cheek offer
also the other; and him that taketh away thy cloak forbid not
to take thy coat also.

Give to every man that asketh of thee; and of him that
taketh away thy goods ask them not again.

And as ye would that men should do to you, do ye also to
them likewise.

For if ye love them which love you, what thank have ye?
for sinners also love those that love them.

And if ye do good to them which do good to you, what
thank have ye? for sinners also do even the same.

And if ye lend to them of whom ye hope to receive, what
thank have ye? for sinners also lend to sinners, to receive as
much again.

But love ye your enemies, and do good, and lend, hoping for nothing again; and your reward shall be great, and ye shall be the children of the Highest: for he is kind unto the unthankful and to the evil.

Be ye therefore merciful, as your Father also is merciful.
—*Luke 6:27–36*

LIVE PEACEABLY

Do all things without murmurings and disputings:

That ye may be blameless and harmless, the sons of God, without rebuke, in the midst of a crooked and perverse nation, among whom you shine as lights in the world.
—*Philippians 2:14–15*

Recompense to no man evil for evil. Provide things honest in the sight of all men.

If it be possible, as much as lieth in you, live peaceably with all men.

Dearly beloved, avenge not yourselves, but rather give place unto wrath: for it is written, Vengeance is mine; I will repay, saith the Lord.
—*Romans 12:17–19*

PUBLIC DECENCY

The Bible is a book with a profound social orientation. How humans should relate to one another to achieve the experience of community is a subject to which it returns time and time again. The following passages illustrate its concern for ordinary human decency. Without decency humanity fails not only in fulfilling specific mandates of God but also fails in achieving the more general mandate to create a good and viable social order.

AGAINST FALSEHOOD

Thou shalt not raise a false report: put not thine hand with the wicked to be an unrighteous witness.
—*Exodus 23:1*

These six things doth the Lord hate: yea, seven are an abomination to him: A proud look, a lying tongue, and hands that shed innocent blood, a heart that deviseth wicked imaginations, feet that be swift in running to mischief, a false witness that speaketh lies, and he that soweth discord among brethren.
—*Proverbs 6:16–19*

These are the things that ye shall do; Speak ye every man the truth to his neighbor; execute the judgment of truth and peace in your gates: and let none of you imagine evil in your hearts against his neighbor; and love no false oath: for all these are things that I hate, saith the Lord.
—*Zechariah 8:16–17*

Oh that my head were waters, and mine eyes a fountain of tears, that I might weep day and night for the slain of the daughter of my people!
Oh that I had in the wilderness a lodging place of wayfaring men; that I might leave my people, and go from them! for they be all adulterers, an assembly of treacherous men.
And they bend their tongues like their bow for lies: but they are not valiant for the truth upon the earth; for they proceed from evil to evil, and they know not me saith the Lord.

Take ye heed every one of his neighbor, and trust ye not in any brother: for every brother will utterly supplant, and every neighbor will walk with slanders.

And they will deceive every one his neighbor, and will not speak the truth: they have taught their tongue to speak lies, and weary themselves to commit iniquity.

Thine habitation is in the midst of deceit; through deceit they refuse to know me, saith the Lord.

Therefore thus saith the Lord of hosts, Behold, I will melt them, and try them; for how shall I do for the daughter of my people?

Their tongue is as an arrow shot out; it speaketh deceit: one speaketh peaceably to his neighbor with his mouth, but in his heart he layeth his wait.

Shall I not visit them for these things? saith the Lord: shall not my soul be avenged on such a nation as this?
—*Jeremiah 9:1–9*

And be renewed in the spirit of your mind;

And that ye put on the new man, which after God is created in righteousness and true holiness.

Wherefore putting away lying, speak every man truth with this neighbor: for we are members one of another.

Be ye angry, and sin not: let not the sun go down upon your wrath.
—*Ephesians 4:23–26*

AGAINST CHEATING

Ye shall do no unrighteousness in judgment, in mete-yard, in weight, or in measure. Just balances, just weights, a just ephah, and a just hin, shall ye have: I am the Lord your God, which brought you out of the land of Egypt.
—*Leviticus 19:35–36*

Cursed be he that removeth his neighbor's landmark: and all people shall say, Amen.
—*Deuteronomy 27:17*

A false balance is abomination to the Lord: but a just weight his delight.
—*Proverbs 11:1*

Hear this, O ye that swallow up the needy, even to make the poor of the land to fail,

Saying, When will the new moon be gone, that we may sell corn? and the sabbath, that we may set forth wheat, making the ephah small, and the shekel great, and falsifying the balances by deceit?

That we may buy the poor for silver, and the needy for a pair of shoes; yea, and sell the refuse of the wheat?

That Lord hath sworn by the excellency of Jacob, Surely I will never forget any of their works.

—Amos 8:4–7

Are there yet the treasures of wickedness in the house of the wicked, and the scant measure that is abominable?

Shall I count them pure with the wicked balances, and with the bag of deceitful weights?

For the rich men thereof are full of violence, and the inhabitants thereof have spoken lies, and their tongue is deceitful in their mouth.

Therefore also will I make thee sick in smiting thee, in making thee desolate because of thy sins.

Thou shalt eat, but not be satisfied; and they casting down shall be in the midst of thee; and thou shalt take hold, but shalt not deliver; and that which thou deliverest will I give up to the sword.

Thou shalt sow, but thou shalt not reap; thou shalt tread the olives, but thou shalt not anoint thee with oil; and sweet wine, but shalt not drink wine.

—Micah 6:10–15

Then came also publicans to be baptized, and said unto John the Baptist, Master, what shall we do?

And he said unto them, Exact no more than that which is appointed you.

—*Luke 3:12–13*

ON SHARING

When thou comest into thy neighbor's vineyard, then thou mayest eat grapes they fill at thine own pleasure; but thou shalt not put any in thy vessel.

When thou comest into the standing corn of thy neighbor, then thou mayest pluck the ears with thine hand; but thou shalt not move a sickle unto thy neighbor's standing corn.

—*Deuteronomy 23:24–25*

HELP THE HANDICAPPED

Cursed be he that maketh the blind to wander out of the way. And all the people shall say, Amen.

—*Deuteronomy 27:18*

ON EXPLOITATION

Why, seeing times are not hidden from the Almighty, do they that know him not see his days?

Some remove the landmarks; they violently take away flocks, and feed thereof.

They drive away the ass of the fatherless, they take the widow's ox for a pledge.

They turn the needy out of the way: the poor of the earth hide themselves together.

Behold, as wild asses in the desert, go they forth to their work; rising betimes for a prey: the wilderness yieldeth food for them and for their children.

They reap every one his corn in the field: and they gather the vintage of the wicked.

They cause the naked to lodge without clothing, that they have no covering in the cold.

They are wet with the showers of the mountains, and embrace the rock for want of a shelter.

They pluck the fatherless from the breast, and take a pledge of the poor.

The cause him to go naked without clothing, and they take away the sheaf from the hungry;

Which make oil within their walls, and tread their wine-presses, and suffer thirst.

—*Job 24:1–11*

Woe unto him that buildeth his house by unrighteousness, and his chambers by wrong; that useth his neighbor's service without wages, and giveth him not for his work;

That saith, I will build me a wide house and large chambers, and cutteth him out windows; and it is ceiled with cedar, and painted with vermilion.

Shalt thou reign, because thou closest thyself in cedar? did not thy father eat and drink, and do judgment and justice, and then it was well with him?

He judged the cause of the poor and needy; then it was well with him: was not this to know me? saith the Lord.

But thine eyes and thine heart are not but for thy covetousness, and for to shed innocent blood, and for oppression, and for violence, to do it.

Therefore thus saith the Lord concerning Jehoiakim the son of Josiah king of Judah: They shall not lament for him, saying, Ah my brother! or Ah sister! they shall not lament for him, saying Ah lord! or, Ah his glory!

He shall be buried with the burial of an ass, drawn and cast forth beyond the gates of Jerusalem.

—*Jeremiah 22:13–19*

Woe to them that devise iniquity, and work evil upon their beds! when the morning is light, they practice it, because it is in the power of their hand.

And they covet fields, and take them by violence; and houses, and take them away; so they oppress a man and his house, even a man and his heritage.

—*Micah 2:1–2*

And the soldiers likewise demanded of John the Baptist, saying And what shall we do? And he said unto them, Do violence to no man, neither accuse any falsely; and be content with your wages.

—*Luke 3:14*

ON HONOR

Lord, who shall abide in thy tabernacle? Who shall dwell in thy holy hill?

He that walketh uprightly, and worketh righteousness, and speaketh the truth in his heart.

He that backbiteth not with his tongue, nor doeth evil to his neighbor, nor taketh up a reproach against his neighbor.

In whose eyes a vile person is contemned; but he honoreth them that fear the Lord. He that sweareth to his own hurt, and changeth not.

He that putteth not out his money to usury, nor taketh reward against the innocent. He that doeth these things shall never be moved.

—*Psalm 15*

PUBLIC TRUTH

George Orwell observed that the degeneration of society could be measured by the general corruption of its political speech. The lies that the U.S. government has been foisting on the citizens of America—from Vietnam through Watergate through the Iran Contra affair—attest to the validity of Orwell's propositions. However, Orwell was not the first to emphasize the importance of honest public dialogue. Concern for these matters was raised by the prophets Jeremiah and Ezekiel in evaluating the political orders of their times.

SOLOMON

He that speaketh truth sheweth forth righteousness: but a false witness deceit.
. . . The lip of truth shall be established forever: but a lying tongue is but for a moment.
—*Proverbs 12:17, 19*

For from the least of them even unto the greatest of them every one is given to covetousness; and from the prophet even unto the priest every one dealeth falsely.

They have healed also the hurt of the daughter of my people slightly, saying, Peace, peace; when there is no peace.
—*Jeremiah 6:13–14*

Then the Lord said unto me, The prophet's prophesy lies in my name: I sent them not, neither have I commanded them, neither spake unto them: they prophesy unto you a false vision and divination, and a thing of nought, and the deceit of their heart.

Therefore thus saith the Lord concerning the prophets that prophesy in my name, I sent them not, yet they say, Sword and famine shall not be in this land; By sword and famine shall those prophets be consumed.
—*Jeremiah 14:14–15*

For among my people are found wicked men: they lay wait, as he that setteth snares; they set a trap, they catch men.

As a cage is full of birds, so are their houses full of deceit: therefore they are become great, and waxen rich.

They are waxen fat, they shine: yea, the overpass the deeds of the wicked: they judge not the cause, the cause of the fatherless, yet they prosper; and the right of the needy do they not judge.

Shall I not visit for these things? saith the Lord: shall not my soul be avenged on such a nation as this?

A wonderful and horrible thing is committed in the land;

The prophets prophesy falsely, and the priests bear rule by their means; and my people love to have it so: and what will ye do in the end thereof?
—*Jeremiah 5:26–31*

EZEKIEL

Therefore saith the Lord God; Because ye have spoken vanity, and seen lies, therefore, behold, I am against you, saith the Lord God.

And mine hand shall be upon the prophets that see vanity, and that divine lies: they shall not be in the assembly of my people, neither shall they be written in the writing of the house of Israel, neither shall they enter into the land of Israel; and ye shall know that I am the Lord God.

Because, even because they have seduced my people, saying, Peace; and there was no peace . . .
—*Ezekiel 13:8–10*

RESPECT FOR THE ENVIRONMENT

By stating that man should go and subdue the earth the Bible has frequently been blamed for the ravage of the environment perpetrated by western civilization. However, the following passages suggest that man should show as much concern for their earthly furnishings as for the other home in heaven awaiting them after death.

. . . IN PEACE

Six years thou shalt sow thy field, and six years thou shalt prune thy vineyard, and gather in the fruit thereof;

But in the seventh year shall be a sabbath of rest unto the land, a sabbath for the Lord: thou shalt neither sow thy field, nor prune thy vineyard.

That which groweth of its own accord of thy harvest thou shalt not reap, neither gather the grapes of thy vine undressed: for it is a year of rest unto the land.

—*Leviticus 25:3–5*

. . . AND IN WAR

When thou shalt beseige a city a long time, in making war against it to take it, thou shalt not destroy the trees thereof by forcing an ax against them: for thou mayest eat of them, and thou shalt not cut them down (for the tree of the field is man's life) to employ them in the siege.

—*Deuteronomy 20:19*

RESPECT FOR WOMEN

Since the Bible was composed by writers who lived in patriarchal societies, it should not be surprising that it has a reputation for a certain amount of sexism. What is more surprising, however, is the way that reputation is employed to perpetuate sexism today. Sexists cite certain biblical passages to justify the subordination of women at home and in public life. While they accept the authority of the Bible in these areas, they ignore or reject it when the Bible's sexism extends to matters like polygamy. A number of the men of God had a number of wives, yet the sexists refrain from promoting a recapitulation of these moral examples. In short, the sexists select what Bible passages they like, and reject those they find to conflict with their interests.

In actuality the Bible also contains passages which evidence a more progressive consciousness. Women organize, lead, and have the right to hold property. As Susan Jacoby has demonstrated (*Wild Justice*, Harper & Row, 1983), Exodus contains legal provisions implying that a fetus is something less than the full-fledge human being the anti-abortionists believe it to be. An assault that results in a miscarriage generates a penalty determined by the husband and judges, but the penalty does not rise to the level of eye for eye (or life for life) unless the pregnant woman suffers more than a miscarriage. Similarly, Richard Freidman (*Who Wrote the Bible?*, Summit Books, 1987) has drawn attention to Deuteronomy's concern for the enemy women, who are likely to be raped. If an Israelite soldier desires a woman from among the enemy he must allow her to mourn before he may have sex with her. After that he must marry her or release her. The Gospel narrative indicates the important role that women play in the value system of Jesus, as it was to a woman that he first appeared after his death.

In the end what should impress us is not the extent to which Biblical writers were limited by the patriarchal notions of their times, but rather, the extent to which they were able to transcend them.

EQUALITY AS THE GOAL

There is neither Jew nor Greek, there is neither bond nor free, there is neither male nor female: for ye are all one in Christ Jesus.
—*Galatians 3:28*

A WOMAN LEADS EFFECTIVELY

And Deborah, a prophetess, the wife of Lapidoth, she judged Israel at that time.

And she dwelt under the palm tree of Deborah between Ramah and Beth-el in mount Ephraim: and the children of Israel came up to her for judgment.

And she sent and called Barak the son of Abinoam out of Kedesh-naphtali, and said unto him, Hath not the Lord God of Israel commanded, saying, Go and draw toward mount Tabor, and take with thee ten thousand men of the children of Naphtali and of the children of Zebulun?

And I will draw unto thee to the river Kishon, Sisera, the captain of Jabin's army, with his chariots and his multitude; and I will deliver him into thine hand.

And Barak said unto her, If thou wilt go with me, then I will go: but if thou wilt not go with me, then I will not go.

And she said: I will surely go with thee, notwithstanding the journey that thou takest shall not be for thy honor; for the Lord will give Sisera over into the hand of a woman.
—*Judges 4:4–9*

WOMEN ORGANIZE

Then came the daughters of Zelophehad, the son of Hepher, the son of Gilead, the son of Machir, the son of Manasseh, of the families of Manasseh the son of Joseph: and these are the names of his daughters; Mahlah, Noah, and Hoglah, and Milcah, and Tirzah.

And they stood before Moses, and before Eleazar the priest, and before the princes and all the congregation, by the door of the tabernacle of the congregations, saying,

Our father died in the wilderness, and he was not in the company of them that gathered themselves together against the Lord in the company of Korah; but died in his own sin, and had no sons.

Why should the name of our father be done away from among his family, because he hath no son? Give unto us therefore a possession among the brethren of our father.

And Moses brought their cause before the Lord.
—*Numbers 27:1–5*

THE RIGHT OF WOMEN TO INHERIT PROPERTY

And the Lord spake unto Moses, saying,

The daughters of Zelophehad speak right: thou shalt surely give them a possession of an inheritance among their father's brethren; and thou shalt cause the inheritance of their father to pass unto them.

And thou shalt speak unto the children of Israel saying, If a man die, and have no son, then ye shall cause his inheritance to pass unto his daughter.
—*Numbers 27:6–8*

A FETUS IS NOT A PERSON

If men strive, and hurt a woman with child, so that her fruit depart from her, and yet no mischief follow: he shall surely be punished, according as the woman's husband will lay upon him; and he shall pay as the judges determine.

And if any mischief follow, then thou shalt give life for life,

Eye for eye, tooth for tooth, hand for hand, foot for foot,

Burning for burning, wound for wound, stripe for stripe.
—*Exodus 21:22–25*

PROVISIONS AGAINST RAPE

When thou goest forth to war against thine enemies, and the Lord thy God hath delivered them into thine hands, and thou hast taken them captive,

And seest among the captives a beautiful woman, and hast a desire unto her, that thou wouldest have her to thy wife;

Then thou shalt bring her home to thine house; and she shall shave her head, and pare her nails;

And she shall put the raiment of her captivity from off her, and shall remain in thine house, and bewail her father and her mother a full month: and after that thou shalt go in unto her, and be her husband, and she shall be thy wife.

And it shall be, if thou have no delight in her, then thou shalt let her go whither she will; but thou shalt not sell her at all for money, thou shalt not make merchandise of her, because thou hast humbled her.
—*Deuteronomy 21:10–14*

THE RESURRECTION'S FIRST WITNESS

The first day of the week cometh Mary Magdalene early, when it was yet dark, unto the sepulchre, and seeth the stone taken away from the sepulchre.

The she runneth, and cometh to Simon Peter, and to the other disciple, whom Jesus loved, and saith unto them, They have taken away the Lord out of the sepulchre, and we know not where they have laid him.

Peter therefore went forth, and that other disciple, and came to the sepulchre. . . .

. . . Then the disciples went away again unto their own home.

But Mary stood without at the sepulchre weeping: and as she wept, she stooped down and looked into the sepulchre.

And seeth two angels in white sitting, the one at the head, and the other at the feet, where the body of Jesus had lain.

And they say unto her, Woman, why weepest thou? She saith unto them, because they have taken away my Lord, and I know not where they have laid him.

And when she had thus said, she turned herself back, and saw Jesus standing, and knew not that it was Jesus.

Jesus saith unto her, Woman, why weepest thou? whom seekest thou? She, supposing him to be the gardener, saith unto him, Sir, if thou have borne him hence, tell me where thou hast laid him, and I will take him away.

Jesus saith unto her, Mary. She turned herself, and saith unto him, Rabboni; which is to say, Master.

Jesus saith unto her, Touch me not; for I am not yet ascended to my Father: but go to my brethren, and say unto them, I ascend unto my Father, and your Father; and to my God, and to your God.

Mary Magdalene came and told the disciples that she had seen the Lord, and that he had spoken these things unto her.

—*John 20:1–3, 10–18*

RESPECT FOR MINORITIES

From the Old Testament through the New the Bible stresses that all humans belong to the same family. Discrimination against those who are different, foreign, or from another ethnic group may be an all-too-human predisposition but from a Biblical standpoint, it is utterly reprehensible.

AGAINST DISCRIMINATION

Thou shalt neither vex a stranger, nor oppress him: for ye were strangers in the land of Egypt.
—*Exodus 22:21*

Also thou shalt not oppress a stranger: for ye know the heart of a stranger, seeing ye were strangers in the land of Egypt.
—*Exodus 23:9*

And if a stranger sojourn with thee in your land, ye shall not vex him.
But the stranger that dwelleth with you shall be unto you as one born among you, and thou shalt love him as thyself; for ye were strangers in the land of Egypt: I am the Lord your God.
—*Leviticus 19:33–34*

Then Peter opened his mouth, and said, Of a truth I perceive that God is no respecter of persons:
But in every nation he that feareth him, and worketh righteousness, is accepted with him.
—*Acts 10:34–35*

But he, willing to justify himself, said unto Jesus, And who is my neighbor?
And Jesus answering said, A certain man went down from Jerusalem to Jericho, and fell among thieves, which stripped him of his raiment, and wounded him, and departed, leaving him half dead.
And by chance there came down a certain priest that way: and when he saw him, he passed by on the other side.

38

And likewise a Levite, when he was at the place, came and looked on him, and passed by on the other side.

But a certain Samaritan, as he journeyed, came where he was: and when he saw him, he had compassion on him,

And went to him, and bound up his wounds, pouring in oil and wine, and set him on his own beast, and brought him to an inn, and took care of him.

And on the morrow when he departed, he took out two pence, and gave them to the host, and said unto him, Take care of him; and whatsoever thou spendest more, when I come again, I will repay thee.

Which now of these three, thinkest thou, was neighbor unto him that fell among the thieves?

And he said, He that sheweth mercy on him. Then said Jesus unto him, and do thou likewise.
—*Luke 10:29–37*

EQUAL PROTECTION UNDER THE LAW

Ye shall have one manner of law, as well for the stranger, as for one of your own country: for I am the Lord your God.
—*Leviticus 24:22*

One ordinance shall be both for you of the congregation, and also for the stranger that sojourneth with you, an ordinance for ever in your generations: as ye are, so shall the stranger be before the Lord.

One law and one manner shall be for you, and for the stranger that sojourneth with you.
—*Numbers 15:15–16*

BLACK IS BEAUTIFUL

I am black, but comely, O ye daughters of Jerusalem, as the tents of Kedar, as the curtains of Solomon.
—*Song of Solomon, 1:5*

RESPECT FOR JUSTICE

The Bible's emphasis on political theory is most pronounced in its statements concerning the implementation of justice. Not content with mere celebrations of abstract justice, the Biblical prophets and kings were more concerned with judicial issues in concrete situations. The basic fairness of a society's legal system speaks to its essential success or failure as a human community. The number of Biblical writers who address this issue attest to its fundamental importance. Perhaps of greatest interest are the assertions of Isaiah, which equate the sins of Sodom and Gomorrah to the practices of corrupt judges. In other words, the cities which have become metaphors for ultimate evil stand condemned not for sexual excess but for the lack of integrity that undermined their legal systems.

MOSES

Cursed be he that perverteth the judgment of the stranger, fatherless, and widow. And all the people shall say, Amen.
—*Deuteronomy 27:19*

DAVID

Give the king thy judgments, O God, and thy righteousness unto the king's son.

He shall judge thy people with righteousness, and thy poor with judgment.

The mountains shall bring peace to the people, and the little hills, by righteousness.

He shall judge the poor of the people, he shall save the children of the needy, and shall break in pieces the oppressor. . . .

. . . For he shall deliver the needy when he crieth; the poor also, and him that hath no helper.

He shall spare the poor and needy, and shall save the souls of the needy.

He shall redeem their soul from deceit and violence: and precious shall their blood be in his sight.
—*Psalms 72:1-4, 12-14*

God standeth in the congregation of the mighty; he judgeth among the gods.

How long will ye judge unjustly, and accept the persons of the wicked? Selah.

Defend the poor and fatherless: do justice to the afflicted and needy.

Deliver the poor and needy: rid them out of the hand of the wicked.

They know not, neither will they understand; they walk on in darkness: all the foundations of the earth are out of course.

I have said, Ye are gods; and all of you are children of the Most High.

But ye shall die like men, and fall like one of the princes.

Arise, O God, judge the earth: for thou shalt inherit all nations.

—Psalms 82

O Lord God, to whom vengeance belongeth; O God, to whom vengeance belongeth, show thyself.

Lift up thyself, thou judge of the earth: render a reward to the proud.

Lord, how long shall the wicked, how long shall the wicked triumph?

How long shall they utter and speak hard things? and all the works of iniquity boast themselves?

They break in pieces thy people, O Lord, and afflict thine heritage.

They slay the widow and the stranger, and murder the fatherless.

Yet they say, The Lord shall not see, neither shall the God of Jacob regard it.

Understand, ye brutish among the people: and ye fools, when will ye be wise?

He that planted the ear, shall he not hear? He that formed the eye, shall he not see?

He that chastiseth the heathen, shall not he correct? He that teacheth man knowledge, shall not he know?

The Lord knoweth the thoughts of man, that they are vanity.

Blessed is the man whom thou chasteneth, O Lord, and teachest him out of thy law;

41

That thou mayest give him rest from the days of adversity, until the pit be digged for the wicked.

For the Lord will not cast off his people, neither will he forsake his inheritance.

But judgment shall return unto righteousness: and all the upright in heart shall follow it.

Who will rise up for me against the evildoers? Or who will stand up for me against the workers of iniquity?

Unless the Lord had been my help, my soul had almost dwelt in silence.

When I said, My foot slippeth; thy mercy, O Lord, held me up.

In the multitude of my thoughts within me thy comforts delight my soul.

Shall the throne of iniquity have fellowship with thee, which frameth mischief by a law?

They gather themselves together against the soul of the righteous, and condemn the innocent blood.

But the Lord is my defense; and my God is the rock of my refuge.

And he shall bring upon them their own iniquity, and shall cut them off in their own wickedness; yea, the Lord our God shall cut them off.

—*Psalms 94*

ISAIAH

Hear the word of the Lord, ye rulers of Sodom; give ear unto the law of our God, ye people of Gomorrah.

To what purpose is the multitude of your sacrifices unto me? saith the Lord: I am full of the burnt offerings of rams, and the fat of fed beasts; and I delight not in the blood of bullocks, or of lambs, or of he goats.

When ye come to appear before me, who hath required this at your hand, to tread my courts?

Bring no more vain oblations; incense is an abomination unto me; the new moons and sabbaths, the calling of assemblies, I cannot away with; it is iniquity, even the solemn meeting.

Your new moons and your appointed feasts my soul hateth: they are a trouble to me; I am weary to bear them.

And when ye spread forth your hands, I will hide mine

eyes from you; yea, when ye make many prayers, I will not hear: your hands are full of blood.

Wash ye, make you clean; put away the evil of your doings from before mine eyes; cease to do evil;

Learn to do well; seek judgment, relieve the oppressed, judge the fatherless, plead for the widow.
—*Isaiah 1:10–17*

Woe unto them that decree unrighteous decrees, and that write grievousness which they have prescribed;

To turn aside the needy from judgment, and to take away the right from the poor of my people, that widows may be their prey, and that they may rob the fatherless!
—*Isaiah 10:1–2*

JEREMIAH

Thus saith the Lord of hosts, the God of Israel, Amend your ways and your doings, and I will cause you to dwell in this place.

Trust ye not in lying words, saying, The temple of the Lord, The temple of the Lord, The temple of the Lord, are these.

For if ye throughly amend your ways and your doings; if ye thoroughly execute judgment between a man and his neighbor;

If ye oppress not the stranger, the fatherless, and the widow, and shed not innocent blood in this place, neither walk after other gods to your hurt;

Then will I cause you to dwell in this place, in the land that I gave to your fathers, for ever and ever.

Behold, ye trust in lying words, that cannot profit.
—*Jeremiah 7:3–8*

And touching the house of the king of Judah, say, Hear ye the word of the Lord;

O house of David, thus saith the Lord; Execute judgment in the morning, and deliver him that is spoiled out of the hand of the oppressor, lest my fury go out like fire, and burn that none can quench it, because of the evil of your doings.
—*Jeremiah 21:11–12*

AMOS

Seek the Lord, and ye shall live; lest he break out like fire in the house of Joseph, and devour it, and there be none to quench it in Beth-el.

Ye who turn judgment to wormwood, and leave off righteousness in the earth,

Seek him that maketh the seven stars and Orion, and turneth the shadow of death into the morning, and maketh the day dark with night: that calleth for the waters of the sea, and poureth them out upon the face of the earth: The Lord is his name:

That strengtheneth the spoiled against the strong, so that the spoiled shall come against the fortress.

They hate him that rebuketh in the gate, and they abhor him that speaketh uprightly.

Forasmuch therefore as your treading is upon the poor, and ye take from him burdens of wheat: ye have built houses of hewn stone, but ye shall not dwell in them; ye have planted pleasant vineyards, but ye shall not drink wine of them.

For I know your manifold transgressions and your mighty sins: they afflict the just, they take a bribe, and they turn aside the poor in the gate from their right.
—*Amos 5:6–12*

HABAKKUK

The burden which Habakkuk the prophet did see.

O Lord, how long shall I cry, and thou wilt not hear! even cry out unto thee of violence, and thou wilt not save!

Why dost thou show me iniquity, and cause me to behold grievance? for spoiling and violence are before me: and there are that raise up strife and contention.

Therefore the law is slacked, and judgment doth never go forth: for the wicked doth compass about the righteous; therefore wrong judgment proceedeth.
—*Habakkuk 1:1–4*

MICHAH

Hear this, I pray you, ye heads of the house of Jacob, and princes of the house of Israel, that abhor judgment, and pervert all equity.

44

They build up Zion with blood, and Jerusalem with iniquity.

The heads thereof judge for reward, and the priests thereof teach for hire, and the prophets thereof divine for money: yet will they lean upon the Lord, and say, Is not the Lord among us? none evil can come upon us.

Therefore shall Zion for your sake be plowed as a field, and Jerusalem shall become heaps, and the mountain of the house as the high places of the forest.
—*Micah 3:9–12*

Woe is me! for I am as when they have gathered the summer fruits, as the grape gleanings of the vintage: there is no cluster to eat: my soul desired the first ripe fruit.

The good man is perished out of the earth: and there is none upright among men: they all lie in wait for blood; they hunt every man his brother with a net.

That they may do evil with both hands earnestly, the prince asketh, and the judge asketh for a reward; and the great man, he uttereth his mischievous desire: so they wrap it up.
—*Micah 7:1–3*

JESUS

Woe unto you, scribes and Pharisees, hypocrites! for ye pay tithe of mint and anise and cummin, and have omitted the weightier matters of the law, judgment, mercy, and faith: these ought ye to have done, and not to leave the other undone.

Ye blind guides, which strain at a gnat, and swallow a camel.

Woe unto you, scribes and Pharisees, hypocrites! for ye make clean the outside of the cup and of the platter, but within they are full of extortion and excess.

Thou blind Pharisee, cleanse first that which is within the cup and platter, that the outside of them may be clean also.
—*Matthew 23:23–26*

SOCIAL JUSTICE: AGAINST THE EXPLOITATION OF THE POOR

The Bible's concern with social justice is expressed throughout in a variety of circumstances. Repeatedly it asserts the simple proposition that those in high places should not use their positions of power to exploit the underprivileged.

MOSES

Ye shall not afflict any widow, or fatherless child.

If thou afflict them in any wise, and they cry at all unto me, I will surely hear their cry.
—*Exodus 22:22–23*

Thou shalt not wrest the judgment of thy poor in his cause.
—*Exodus 23:6*

Thous shalt not pervert the judgment of the stranger, nor of the fatherless; nor take a widow's raiment to pledge.
—*Deuteronomy 24:17*

DAVID

Why standest thou afar off, O Lord? why hidest thyself in times of trouble?

The wicked in his pride doth persecute the poor: let them be taken in the devices that they have imagined.

For the wicked boasteth of his heart's desire, and blesseth the covetous, whom the Lord abhorreth.

The wicked, through the pride of his countenance, will not seek after God: God is not in all his thoughts.

His ways are always grievous; thy judgments are far above out of his sight: as for all his enemies, he puffeth at them.

He hath said in his heart, I shall not be moved: for I shall never be in adversity.

His mouth is full of cursing and deceit and fraud: under his tongue is mischief and vanity.

He sitteth in the lurking places of the villages: in the secret places doth he murder the innocent: his eyes are privily set against the poor.

46

He lieth in wait secretly as a lion in his den: he lieth in wait to catch the poor: he doth catch the poor, when he draweth him into his net.

He croucheth, and humbleth himself, that the poor may fall by his strong ones.

He hath said in his heart, God hath forgotten: he hideth his face; he will never see it.

Arise, O Lord; O God, lift up thine hand: forget not the humble.

Wherefore doth the wicked contemn God? He hath said in his heart, Thou wilt not require it.

Thou hast seen it; for thou beholdest mischief and spite, to requite it with thy hand: the poor committeth himself unto thee; thou art the helper of the fatherless.

Break thou the arm of the wicked and the evil man: seek out his wickedness till thou find none.

The Lord is King for ever and ever: the heathen are perished out of his land. Lord, thou hast heard the desire of the humble: thou wilt prepare their heart, thou wilt cause thine ear to hear:

To judge the fatherless and the oppressed, that the man of the earth may no more oppress.
—*Psalms 10*

SOLOMON

He that oppresseth the poor reproacheth his Maker: but he that honoreth him hath mercy on the poor.
—*Proverbs 14:31*

Rob not the poor, because he is poor: neither oppress the afflicted in the gate:

For the Lord will plead their cause, and spoil the soul of those that spoiled them.
—*Proverbs 22:22–23*

Remove not the old landmark; and enter not into the fields of the fatherless:

For their Redeemer is mighty; he shall plead their cause with thee.
—*Proverbs 23:10–11*

ISAIAH

The Lord standeth up to plead, and standeth to judge the people.

The Lord will enter into judgment with the ancients of his people, and the princes thereof: for ye have eaten up the vineyard; the spoil of the poor is in your houses.

What mean ye that ye beat my people to pieces, and grind the faces of the poor? saith the Lord God of hosts.
—*Isaiah 3:13–15*

The instruments also of the churl are evil: he deviseth wicked devices to destroy the poor with lying words, even when the needy speaketh right.
—*Isaiah 32:7*

JEREMIAH

Thus saith the Lord; Execute ye judgment and righteousness, and deliver the spoiled out of the hand of the oppressor: and do no wrong, do no violence to the stranger, the fatherless, nor the widow, neither shed innocent blood in this place.
—*Jeremiah 22:3*

EZEKIEL

Moreover the word of the Lord came unto me saying, Now, thou son of man, wilt thou judge, wilt thou judge the bloody city? yea, thou shalt show her all her abominations. In thee have they taken gifts to shed blood; thou hast taken usury and increase, and thou hast greedily gained of their neighbors by extortion, and hast forgotten me, saith the Lord God. . . . The people of the land have used oppression, and exercised robbery, and have vexed the poor and needy: yea, they have oppressed the stranger wrongfully.
—*Ezekiel 22:1–2, 12, 29*

AMOS

Thus saith the Lord; For three transgressions of Israel, and for four, I will not turn away the punishment thereof; because they sold the righteous for silver, and the poor for a pair of shoes; that pant after the dust of the earth on the head of the poor . . . and turn aside the way of the meek . . .
—*Amos 2:6–7*

Hear this word, ye kine of Bashan, that are in the mountain of Samaria, which oppress the poor, which crush the needy, which say to their masters, Bring, and let us drink.

The Lord God hath sworn by his holiness, that, lo, the days shall come upon you, that he will take you away with hooks, and your posterity with fishhooks.
—*Amos 4:1–2*

MALACHI

And I will come near to you to judgment; and I will be a swift witness against the sorcerers, and against the adulterers, and against false swearers, and against those that oppress the hireling in his wages, the widow, and the fatherless, and that turn aside the stranger from his right, and fear not me, saith the Lord of hosts.
—*Malachi 3:5*

MICHAH

Woe to them that devise iniquity, and work evil upon their beds! when the morning is light, they practise it, because it is in the power of their hand.

And they covet fields, and take them by violence; and houses, and taken them away: so they oppress a man and his house, even a man and his heritage.
—*Micah 2:1–2*

And there was a great cry of the people and of their wives against the brethren of the Jews.

For there were that said, We, our sons, and our daughters, are many: therefore we take up corn for them, that we may eat, and live.

Some also there were that said, We have mortgaged our lands, vineyards, and houses, that we might buy corn, because of the dearth.

There were also that said, We have borrowed money for the king's tribute, and that upon our lands and vineyards.

Yet now as our flesh is as the flesh of our brethren, our children as their children: and, lo, we bring into bondage our sons and our daughters to be servants, and some of our daughters are brought into bondage already: neither is it in our power to redeem them; for other men have our lands and vineyards.

And I was very angry when I heard their cry, and these words.

Then I consulted with myself, and I rebuked the nobles, and the rulers, and said under them, Ye exact usury, every one of his brother. And I set a great assembly against them.

And I said unto them, We, after our ability, have redeemed our brethren the Jews, which were sold into the heathen; and will ye even sell your brethren? Or shall they be sold unto us? Then held they their peace, and found nothing to answer.

Also I said, It is not good that ye do: ought ye not to walk in the fear of our God because of the reproach of the heathen and our enemies?

I likewise, and my brethren, and my servants, might exact of them money and corn: I pray you, let us leave off this usury.

Restore, I pray you, to them, even this day, their lands, their vineyards, their oliveyards, and their houses, also the hundredth part of the money, and of the corn, the wine, and the oil, that ye exact of them.

Then said they, We will restore them, and will require nothing of them; so will we do as thou sayest. Then I called the priests, and took an oath of them, that they should do according to this promise.

Also I shook my lap, and said, So God shake out every
man from his house, and from his labour, that performeth
not this promise, even thus be he shaken out, and emptied.
And all the congregation said, Amen, and praised the Lord.
And the people did according to this promise.
—*Nehemiah 5:1–13*

JESUS

And he said unto them in his doctrine, Beware of the
scribes, which love to go in long clothing, and love saluta-
tions in the market places,

And the chief seats in the synagogues, and the uppermost rooms at feasts;

Which devour widows' houses, and for a pretense make
long prayers: the same shall receive greater damnation.
—*Mark 12:38–40*

JAMES

Go to now, ye rich men, weep and howl for your miseries
that shall come upon you.

Your riches are corrupted, and your garments are moth-
eaten.

Your gold and silver is cankered; and the rust of them
shall be a witness against you, and shall eat your flesh as it
were fire. Ye have heaped treasure together for the last days.

Behold, the hire of the labourers who have reaped down
your fields, which is of you kept back by fraud, crieth: and
the cries of them which have reaped are entered into the
ears of the Lord of Sabath.

Ye have lived in pleasure of the earth, and been wanton;
ye have nourished your hearts, as in a day of slaughter.

Ye have condemned and killed the just; and he doth not
resist you.
—*James 5:1–6*

SOCIAL JUSTICE: AFFIRMATIVELY AIDING THE UNDERPRIVILEGED

The Bible's concern with social justice does not end at mere prohibitions, enjoining the powerful from exploiting the vulnerable. The Bible also affirms that the rich have obligations to aid the poor. Esther describes the Jews honoring God in their festivals by giving to the poor. For his part, the prophet Ezekiel partially disagreed with Isaiah by suggesting that the quintessential sin of Sodom and Gomorrah lay in their selfishness. They were well-to-do, but they did not use their surplus to help the poor.

Significantly, when Jesus pronounces his parable of the day of final judgment, he does not define the saved and the damned by what catechism they recited while they walked on earth. Rather, salvation or damnation turns on the extent to which the individual saw fit to help "the least of these."

DAVID

Blessed is he that considereth the poor: the Lord will deliver him in time of trouble.

The Lord will preserve him, and keep him alive; and he shall be blessed upon the earth: and thou wilt not deliver him unto the will of his enemies.
—Psalms 41:1–2

SOLOMON

He that despiseth his neighbor sinneth: but he that hath mercy on the poor, happy is he.
—Proverbs 14:21

He that hath pity on the poor lendeth unto the Lord; and that which he hath given will He pay him again.
—Proverbs 19:17

Who so stoppeth his ears at the cry of the poor, he also shall cry himself, but shall not be heard.
—Proverbs 21:13

He that giveth unto the poor shall not lack: but he that hideth his eyes shall have many a curse.
—*Proverbs 28:27*

He that hath a bountiful eye shall be blessed; for he giveth his bread to the poor.
—*Proverbs 22:9*

Open thy mouth, judge righteously, and plead the cause of the poor and needy.
—*Proverbs 31:9*

Who can find a virtuous woman? For her price is far above rubies. . . . she stretcheth out her hand to the poor; yea, she reacheth forth her hands to the needy.
—*Proverbs 31:10, 20*

ESTHER

As the days wherein the Jews rested from their enemies, and the month which was turned unto them from sorrow to joy, and from mourning into a good day: that they should make them days of feasting and joy, and of sending portions one to another, and gifts to the poor.
—*Esther 9:22*

JOB

For thou hast taken a pledge from thy brother for nought, and stripped the naked of their clothing.
Thou hast not given water to the weary to drink, and thou hast withholden bread from the hungry.
—*Job 22:6–7*

I was eyes to the blind, and feet was I to the lame.
I was a father to the poor: and the cause which I knew not I searched out.
—*Job 29:15–16*

If I have withheld the poor from their desire, or have caused the eyes of the widow to fail;
Or have eaten my morsel myself alone, and the fatherless hath not eaten thereof;

53

(For from my youth he was brought up with me, as with a father, and I have guided her from my mother's womb;)

If I have seen any perish for want of clothing, or any poor without covering;

If his loins have not blessed me, and if he were not warmed with the fleece of my sheep;

If I have lifted up my hand against the fatherless, when I saw my help in the gate:

Then let mine arm fall from my shoulder blade, and mine arm be broken from the bone.
—*Job 31:16–22*

EZEKIEL

As I live, saith the Lord God, Sodom thy sister hath not done, she nor her daughters, as thou hast done, thou and thy daughters.

Behold, this was the iniquity of thy sister Sodom, pride, fullness of bread, and abundance of idleness was in her and in her daughters, neither did she strengthen the hand of the poor and needy.
—*Ezekiel 16:48–49*

JOHN THE BAPTIST

And the people asked John the Baptist, What shall we do then?

He answereth and saith unto them, He that hath two coats, let him impart to him that hath none; and he that hath meat, let him do likewise.
—*Luke 3:10–11*

JESUS

There was a certain rich man, which was clothed in purple and fine linen, and fared sumptuously every day:

And there was a certain beggar named Lazarus, which was laid at his gate, full of sores.

And desiring to be fed with the crumbs which fell from the rich man's table: moreover the dogs came and licked his sores.

And it came to pass, that the beggar died, and was carried by the angels into Abraham's bosom: and the rich man also died, and was buried.

54

And in hell he lift up his eyes, being in torments, and seeth Abraham afar off, and Lazarus in his bosom.

And he cried and said, Father Abraham, have mercy on me, and send Lazarus, that he may dip the tip of his finger in water, and cool my tongue; for I am tormented in this flame.

But Abraham said, Son, remember that thou in thy lifetime receivedst thy good things, and likewise Lazarus evil things: but now he is comforted, and thou art tormented.

And beside all this, between us and you there is a great gulf fixed: so that they which would pass from hence to you cannot; neither can they pass to us, that would come from thence.

Then he said, I pray thee therefore, father, that thou wouldst send him to my father's house:

For I have five brethren; that he may testify unto them, lest they also come into this place of torment.

Abraham saith unto him, They have Moses and the prophets; let them hear them.

And he said, Nay, father Abraham: but if one went unto them from the dead, they will repent.

And he said unto him, If they hear not Moses and the prophets, neither will they be persuaded, though one rose from the dead.
—*Luke 16:19–31*

Then said Jesus also to him that bade him, When thou makest a dinner or a supper, call not thy friends, nor thy brethren, neither thy kinsmen, nor thy rich neighbors; lest they also bid thee again, and a recompense be made thee.

But when thou makest a feast, call the poor, the maimed, the lame, the blind:

And thou shalt be blessed; for they cannot recompense thee: for thou shalt be recompensed at the resurrection of the just.
—*Luke 14:12–14*

And as Jesus spake, a certain Pharisee besought him to dine with him: and he went in, and sat down to meat.

And when the Pharisee saw it, he marvelled that he had not first washed before dinner.

And the Lord said unto him, Now do you Pharisees make clean the outside of the cup and the platter; but your inward part is full of ravening and wickedness.

55

Ye fools, did not he, that made that which is without, make that which is within also?

But rather give alms of such things as ye have; and, behold, all things are clean unto you.

—Luke 11:37–41

When the Son of man shall come in his glory, and all the holy angels with him, then shall he sit upon the throne of his glory.

And before him shall be gathered all nations: and he shall separate them one from another, as a shepherd divideth his sheep from the goats:

And he shall set the sheep on his right hand, but the goats on the left.

Then shall the King say unto them on his right hand, Come, ye blessed of my father, inherit the kingdom prepared for you from the foundation of the world:

For I was an hungred, and ye gave me meat: I was thirsty, and ye gave me drink: I was a stranger, and ye took me in:

Naked, and ye clothed me, I was sick, and ye visited me: I was in prison, and ye came unto me.

Then shall the righteous answer him, saying, Lord, when we saw thee an hungred, and fed thee? or thirsty, and gave thee drink?

When we saw thee a stranger, and took thee in? or naked, and clothed thee?

Or when we saw thee sick, or in prison, and came unto thee?

And the King shall answer and say unto them, Verily I say unto you, Inasmuch as ye have done it unto one of the least of these my brethren, you have done it unto me.

Then shall he say also unto them on the left hand, Depart from me, ye cursed, into everlasting fire, prepared for the devil and his angels:

For I was an hungred, and ye gave me no meat: I was thirsty, and ye gave me no drink:

I was a stranger, and ye took me not in: naked, and ye clothed me not: sick, and in prison, and ye visited me not.

Then shall they also answer him, saying, Lord, when saw we thee an hungred, or athirst, or a stranger, or naked, or sick, or in prison, and did not minister unto thee?

Then shall he answer them, saying, Verily I say unto you, Inasmuch as ye have done it not to one of the least of these, ye did it not to me.

And these shall go away into everlasting punishment: but the righteous into life eternal.
—*Matthew 25:31–46*

PAUL

Charge them that are rich in this world, that they be not highminded, nor trust in uncertain riches, but in the living God, who giveth us richly all things to enjoy;

That they do good, that they be rich in good works, ready to distribute, willing to communicate . . .
—*I Timothy 6:17–18*

SOCIAL JUSTICE: ASSURING FAIR PRACTICES

Man's obligation to social justice does not only imply refraining from repression or accomplishing isolated incidents of charity. Instead the objective is a social order which mandates systems that undercut the perpetuation of poverty and exploitation, and vindicate and promote a general sense of decency and generosity. This is manifested in various customs and systems developed throughout the Old and New Testaments: the draft exemption laws of Moses, the share and share alike principle of King David, the communism of Jesus' apostles and so forth.

One of the more intriguing customs is that of the "jubilee," wherein debtors were redeemed from their debts at periodic intervals, so as to undercut radical poverty and curtail further inequities in the distribution of wealth. This system was purportedly enstated by Moses. Throughout the history of the Jews the ruling elite continually attempted to ignore it while their moral leaders attempted to sustain it. The seriousness of the jubilee principle is reflected in the lessons of Jeremiah. The prophet warns the Judeans that God expects them to maintain the jubilee. When they do not, their nation falls to the Babylonians. The ruling classes are deported while the poor are allowed to remain in Judah. As well as illustrating the repercussions of God's judgments, this story depicts the societal breakdown which will occur in a society marked by economic oppression. The poor, having no stake in their country, will fail to support it in times of crisis. The society will collapse. The elite which exploited it to its destruction will vanish.

SHARE AND SHARE ALIKE

And David inquired at the Lord, saying, Shall I pursue after this troop? Shall I overtake them? And He answered him, Pursue: for thou shalt surely overtake them, and without fail recover all.

So David went, he and the six hundred men that were with him, and came to the brook Besor, where those that we left behind stayed. But David pursued, he and four hundred men: for two hundred abode behind, which were so faint that they could not go over the brook Besor. . . .

And David smote the troop he had pursued from the twilight even unto the evening of the next day: and there escaped not a man of them, save four hundred young men, which rode upon camels, and fled.

And David recovered all that the Amalekites had carried away: and David rescued his two wives.

And there was nothing lacking to them, neither small nor great, neither sons nor daughters, neither spoil, nor any thing that they had taken to them: David recovered all.

And David took all the flocks and the herds, which they drave before those other cattle, and said, This is David's spoil.

And David came to the two hundred men, which were so faint that they could not follow David, whom they had made also to abide at the brook Besor: and they went forth to meet David, and to meet the people that were with him: and when David came near to the people, he saluted them.

Then answered all the wicked men and men of Belial, of those that went with David, and said, Because they went not with us, we will not give them aught of the spoil that we have recovered, save to every man his wife and his children, that they may lead them away, and depart.

Then said David, Ye shall not do so, my brethren, with that which the Lord hath given us, who hath preserved us, and delivered the company that came against us into our hand.

For who will hearken unto you in this matter? but as his part is that goeth down to the battle, so shall his part be that tarrieth by the stuff: they shall part alike.

And it was so from that day forward, that he made it a statute and an ordinance for Israel unto this day.
—*I Samuel 30:8–10, 17–25*

And they continued steadfastly in the apostles' doctrine and fellowship, and in breaking of bread, and in prayers.

And fear came upon every soul: and many wonders and signs were done by the apostles.

And all that believed were together, and had all things common;

And sold their possessions and goods, and parted them to all men, as every man had need.

—*Acts 2:42–45*

THE JUBILEE

At the end of every seven years thou shalt make a release.

And this is the manner of the release: Every creditor that lendeth aught unto his neighbor shall release it; he shall not exact it of his neighbour, or of his brother, because it is called the Lord's release.

Of a foreigner thou mayest exact it again; but that which is thine with thy brother thine hand shall release;

Save when there shall be no poor among you; for the Lord shall greatly bless thee in the land which the Lord thy God giveth thee for an inheritance to possess it: . . .

. . . If there be among you a poor man of one of thy brethren within any of the gates in thy land which the Lord thy God giveth thee, thou shalt not harden thine heart, nor shut thine hand from thy poor brother:

But thou shalt open thine hand wide unto him, and shalt surely lend him sufficient for his need, in that which he wanteth.

Beware that there be not a thought in thy wicked heart, saying, The seventh year, the year of release, is at hand; and thine eye be evil against thy poor brother, and thou givest him nought; and he cry unto the Lord against thee, and it be sin unto thee.

Thou shalt surely give him, and thine heart shall not be grieved when thou givest unto him: because that for this thing the Lord thy God shall bless thee in all thy works, and in all that thou puttest thine hand unto.

For the poor shall never cease out of the land: therefore I command thee, saying, Thou shalt open thine hand wide unto thy brother, to thy poor, and to thy needy, in thy land.

—*Deuteronomy 15:1–4, 7–11*

And ye shall hallow the fiftieth year, and proclaim liberty throughout all the land unto all the inhabitants thereof: it shall be a jubilee unto you; and ye shall return every man unto his possession, and ye shall return every man unto his family.

A jubilee shall that fiftieth year be unto you: ye shall not sow, neither reap that which groweth of itself in it, nor gather the grapes in it of thy vine undressed. . . .

. . . Ye shall not therefore oppress one another; but thou shalt fear thy God: for I am the Lord your God. . . .

The land shall not be sold forever: for the land is mine; for ye are strangers and sojourners with me.

And in all the land of your possession ye shall grant a redemption for the land.

If thy brother be waxen poor, and hath sold way some of his possession, and if any of his kin come to redeem it, then shall he redeem that which his brother sold.

And if the man have none to redeem it, and himself be able to redeem it;

Then let him count the years of the sale thereof, and restore the overplus unto the man to whom he sold it; that he may return unto his possession;

But if he be not able to restore it to him, then that which is sold shall remain in the hand of him that hath bought it until the year of jubilee: and in the jubilee it shall go out, and he shall return unto his possession.

And if a man sell a dwelling house in a walled city, then he may redeem it within a whole year after it is sold; within a full year may he redeem it.

And if it be not redeemed within the space of a full year, then the house that is in the walled city shall be established forever to him that bought it throughout his generations: it shall not go out in the jubilee.

But the houses of the villages which have no wall round about them shall be counted as the fields of the country: they may be redeemed, and they shall go out in the jubilee.

Notwithstanding the cities of the Levites, and the houses of the cities of their possession, may the Levites redeem at any time.

And if a man purchase of the Levites, then the house that was sold, and the city of his possession, shall go out in the year of jubilee: for the houses of the cities of the Levites are their possession among the children of Israel.

But the field of the suburbs of their cities may not be sold; for it is their perpetual possession.

And if thy brother be waxen poor, and fallen in decay

with thee; then thou shalt relieve him: yea, though he be a stranger, or a sojourner, that he may live with thee.

Take thou no usury of him, or increase: but fear thy God; that thy brother may live with thee.

Thou shalt not give him thy money upon usury, nor lend him thy victuals for increase.

I am the Lord your God, which brought you forth out of the land of Egypt, to give you the land of Canaan, and to be your God.

And if thy brother that dwelleth with thee be waxen poor, and be sold unto thee; thou shalt not compel him to serve as a bondservant:

But as an hired servant, and as a sojourner, he shall be with thee, and shall serve thee unto the year of jubilee:

And then shall he depart from thee, both he and his children with him, and shall return unto his own family, and unto the possession of his fathers shall he return.

For they are my servants, which I brought forth out of the land of Egypt: they shall not be sold as bondmen.

Thou shalt not rule over him with rigor; but shalt fear thy God.

—*Leviticus 25:10–11, 17, 23–43*

This is the word that came under Jeremiah from the Lord, after that the king Zedekiah had made a covenant with all the people which were at Jerusalem, to proclaim liberty unto them;

That every man should let his manservant, and every man his maidservant, being an Hebrew or a Hebrewess, go free; that none should serve himself of them to wit, of a Jew his brother.

Now when all the princes, and all the people, which had entered into the covenant heard that everyone should let his manservant, and everyone his maidservant, go free, that none should serve themselves of them any more, then they obeyed, and let them go.

But afterwards they turned, and caused the servants and the handmaids, whom they had let go free, to return, and brought them into subjection for servants and for handmaids.

Therefore the word of the Lord came to Jeremiah from the Lord, saying,

Thus saith the Lord, the God of Israel; I made a covenant

with your fathers in the day that I brought them forth out of the land of Egypt, out of the house of bondmen, saying,

At the end of seven years let ye go every man his brother an Hebrew, which hath been sold unto thee; and when he hath served thee six years, thou shalt let him go free from thee: but your fathers hearkened not unto me, neither inclined their ear.

And ye were now turned, and had done right in my sight, in proclaiming liberty every man to his neighbor; and ye had made a covenent before me in the house which is called by my name:

But ye turned and polluted my name, and caused every man his servant, and every man his handmaid, whom he had set at liberty at their pleasure, to return, and brought them into subjection, to be unto you for servants and for handmaids.

Therefore thus saith the Lord; Ye have not hearkened unto me, in proclaiming liberty, every one to his brother, and every man to his neighbor: behold, I proclaim a liberty for you, saith the Lord, to the sword, to the pestilence, and to the famine; and I will make you to be removed into all kingdoms of the earth.

And I will give the men that have transgressed my covenant, which have not performed the words of the covenant which they had made before me, when they cut the calf in twain, and passed between the parts thereof,

The princes of Judah, and the princes of Jerusalem, the enuchs, and the priests, and all the people of the land, which passed between the parts of the calf;

I will even give them into the hand of their enemies, and into the hand of them that seek their life: and their dead bodies shall be for meat unto the fowls of the heaven, and to the beasts of the earth.

And Zedekiah king of Judah and his princes will I give into the hand of their enemies, and into the hand of them that seek their life, and into the hand of the king of Babylon's army, which are gone up from you.

Behold, I will command, saith the Lord, and cause them to return to this city; and they shall fight against it, and take it, and burn it with fire: and I will make the cities of Judah a desolation without an inhabitant.

—*Jeremiah 34:8-22*

GUARANTEED HOLIDAYS

Six days thou shalt work, but on the seventh day thou shalt rest: in earing time and in harvest thou shalt rest.
—*Exodus 34:21*

Six days thou shalt do thy work, and on the seventh day thou shalt rest: that thine ox and thine ass may rest, and the son of thy handmaid, and the stranger, may be refreshed.
—*Exodus 23:12*

DRAFT EXEMPTIONS

When a man hath taken a new wife, he shall not go out to war, neither shall he be charged with any business: but he shall be free at home one year, and shall cheer up his wife which he hath taken.
—*Deuteronomy 24:5*

When thou goest out to battle against thine enemies, and seest horses, and chariots, and a people more than thou, be not afraid of them: for the Lord thy God is with thee, which brought thee out of the land of Egypt.

And it shall be, when ye are come nigh unto the battle, that the priest shall approach and speak unto the people,

And shall say unto them, Hear, O Israel, ye approach this day unto battle against your enemies: let not your hearts faint, fear not, and do not tremble, neither be ye terrified because of them;

For the Lord your God is he that goeth with you, to fight for you against your enemies, to save you.

And the officers shall speak unto the people, saying, What man is there that hath built a new house, and hath not dedicated it? let him go and return to his house, lest he die in the battle, and another man dedicate it.

And what man is he that hath planted a vineyard, and hath not yet eaten of it? let him also go and return unto his house, lest he die in the battle, and another man eat of it.

And what man is he that hath planted a vineyard, and hath not yet eaten of it? let him also go and return unto his house, lest he die in the battle, and another man eat of it.

And what man is there that hath betrothed a wife, and hath not taken her? let him go and return unto his house, lest he die in the battle, and another man take her.

And the officers shall speak further unto the people, and they shall say, What man is there that is fearful and faint-hearted? let him go and return unto his house, lest his brethren's heart faint as well as his heart.

—*Deuteronomy 20:1–8*

SANCTUARIES

When the Lord thy God hath cut off the nations, whose land the Lord thy God giveth thee, and thou succeedest them, and dwellest in their cities, and in their houses;

Thou shalt separate three cities for thee in the midst of thy land, which the Lord thy God giveth thee to possess it.

Thou shalt prepare thee a way, and divide the coasts of thy land, which the Lord thy God giveth thee to inherit, into three parts, that every slayer may flee thither.

And this is the case of the slayer, which shall flee thither, that he may live: Whoso killeth his neighbor igno-rantly, whom he hated not in time past;

As when a man goeth into the wood with his neighbor to hew wood, and his hand fetcheth a stroke with the axe to cut down the tree, and the head slippeth from the helve, and lighteth upon his neighbor, that he die; he shall flee unto one of those cities, and live:

Lest the avenger of the blood pursue the slayer, while his heart is hot, and overtake him, because the way is long, and slay him; whereas he was not worthy of death, inasmuch as he hated him not in time past.

Wherefore I command thee, saying, Thou shalt separate three cities for thee.

And if the Lord thy God enlarge thy coast, as he hath sworn unto thy fathers, and give thee all the land which he promised to give unto thy fathers;

If thou shalt keep all these commandments to do them, which I command thee this day, to love the Lord thy God, and to walk ever in his ways; then shalt thou add three cities more for thee, beside these three:

That innocent blood be not shed in thy land, which the Lord thy God giveth thee for an inheritance, and so blood be upon thee.

But if any man hate his neighbor, and lie in wait for him, and rise up against him, and smite him mortally that he die, and fleeth into one of these cities:

Then the elders of his city shall send and fetch him thence, and deliver him into the hand of the avenger of blood, that he may die.
—*Deuteronomy 19:1–12*

TWO WITNESSES REQUIRED FOR CAPITAL PUNISHMENT

Whoso killeth any person, the murderer shall be put to death by the mouth of witnesses: but one witness shall not testify against any person to cause him to die.
—*Numbers 35:30*

PAY WAGES PROMPTLY

Thou shalt not defraud thy neighbor, neither rob him: the wages of him that is hired shall not abide with thee all night until the morning.
—*Leviticus 19:13*

Thou shalt not oppress a hired servant that is poor and needy, whether he be of thy brethren, or of thy strangers that are in thy land within thy gates:

At his day thou shalt give him his hire, neither shall the sun go down upon it; for he is poor, and setteth his heart

upon it: lest he cry against thee unto the Lord, and it be sin unto thee.
—*Deuteronomy 24:14–15*

LIFELINE RATES

If thou lend money to any of my people that is poor by thee, thou shalt not be to him as a usurer, neither shalt thou lay upon him usury.

If thou at all take thy neighbor's raiment to pledge, thou shalt deliver it unto him by that the sun goeth down:

For that is his covering only, it is his raiment for his skin: wherein shall he sleep? and it shall come to pass, when he crieth unto me, that I will hear; for I am gracious.
—*Exodus 22:25–27*

And the priest shall offer the sin offering, and make an atonement for him that is to be cleansed from his uncleanliness; and afterward he shall kill the burnt offering:

And the priest shall offer the burnt offering and the meat offering upon the altar: and the priest shall make an atonement for him, and he shall be clean.

And if he be poor, and cannot get so much; then he shall take one lamb for a trespass offering to be waved, to make an atonement for him, and one tenth deal of fine flour mingled with oil for a meat offering, and a log of oil;

And two turtledoves, or two young pigeons, such as he is able to get; and the one shall be a sin offering, and the other a burnt offering.
—*Leviticus 14:19–22*

When thou dost lend thy brother any thing, thou shalt not go into his house to fetch his pledge.

Thou shalt stand abroad, and the man to whom thou dost lend shall bring out the pledge abroad unto thee.

And if the man be poor, thou shalt not sleep with his pledge.

In any case thou shalt deliver him the pledge again when the sun goeth down, that he may sleep in his own raiment, and bless thee: and it shall be righteousness unto thee before the Lord thy God.
—*Deuteronomy 24:10–13*

SHARE THE WEALTH

And six years thou shalt sow thy land, and shalt gather in the fruits thereof:

But the seventh year thou shalt let it rest and lie still; that the poor of thy people may eat: and what they leave bhe beasts of the field shall eat. In like manner thou shalt deal with thy vineyard, and with thy oliveyard.
—*Exodus 23:10–11*

And when ye reap the harvest of your land, thou shalt not wholly reap the corners of thy field, neither shalt thou gather the gleanings of thy harvest.

And thou shalt not glean thy vineyard, neither shalt thou gather every grape from thy vineyard; thou shalt leave them for the poor and stranger: I am the Lord your God.
—*Leviticus 19:9–10*

When thou cuttest down thine harvest in thy field, and hast forgot a sheaf in the field, thou shalt not go again to fetch it: it shall be for the stranger, for the fatherless, and for the widow: that the Lord thy God may bless thee in all the work of thine hands.

When thou beatest thine olive tree, thou shalt not go over the boughs again: it shall be for the stranger, for the fatherless, and for the widow.

When thou gatherest the grapes of thy vineyard, thou shalt not glean it afterward: it shall be for the stranger, for the fatherless, and for the widow.
—*Deuteronomy 24:19–21*

Thou shalt not muzzle the ox when he treadeth out the corn.
—*Deuteronomy 25:4*

And with great power gave the apostles witness of the resurrection of the Lord Jesus: and great grace was upon them all.

Neither was there any among them that lacked: for as many as were possessors of lands or houses sold them, and brought the prices of the things that were sold,   And laid them down at the apostles' feet: and distribution was made unto every man according as he had need.
—*Acts 4:33–35*

And in those days, when the number of the disciples was multiplied, there arose a murmuring of the Grecians against the Hebrews, because their widows were neglected in the daily ministration.

Then the twelve called the multitude of the disciples unto them, and said, It is not reason that we should leave the word of God, and serve tables.

Wherefore, brethren, look ye out among you seven men of honest report, full of Holy Ghost and wisdom, whom we may appoint over this business.

But we will give ourselves continually to prayer, and to the ministry of the word.

And the saying pleased the whole multitude: and they chose Stephen, a man full of faith and of the Holy Ghost, and Philip, and Prochorus, and Nicanor, and Timon, and Parmenas, and Nicolas a proselyte of Antioch.
—*Acts 6:1–5*

RESPONSIBILITY ATTENDS PRIVILEGE

But Nebuzaradan the captain of the guard left of the poor of people, which had nothing, in the land of Judah, and gave them vineyards and fields at the same time.
—*Jeremiah 39:10*

Ye that put far away the evil day, and cause the seat of violence to come near;

That lie upon beds of ivory, and stretch themselves upon

their couches, and eat the lambs out of the block, and the calves out of the midst of the stall; that chant to the sound of the viol, and invent to themselves instruments of music, like David;

That drink wine in bowls, and anoint themselves with the chief ointments: but they are not grieved for the affliction of Joseph.

Therefore now shall they go captive with the first that go captive, and the banquet of them that stretched themselves shall be removed.

The Lord God hath sworn by himself, saith the Lord the God of hosts, I abhor the excellency of Jacob, and hate his palaces: therefore will I deliver up the city with all that is therein.

—*Amos 6:3–8*

And the word of the Lord came unto me saying,

Son of man, prophesy against the shepherds of Israel, prophesy, and say unto them, Thus saith the Lord God unto the shepherds; Woe be to the shepherds of Israel that do feed themselves! should not the shepherds feed the flocks?

Ye eat the fat, and ye clothe you with the wool, ye kill them that are fed: but ye feed not the flock.

The diseased have ye not strengthened, neither have ye healed that which was sick, neither have ye bound up that which was broken, neither have ye brought again that which was driven away, neither have ye sought that which was lost; but with force and with cruelty have ye ruled them.

And they were scattered, because there is no shepherds: and they became meat to all the beasts of the field, when they were scattered.

My sheep wandered through all the mountains, and upon every high hill: yea, my flock was scattered upon all the face of the earth, and none did search or seek after them.

Therefore, ye shepherds, hear the word of the Lord;

As I live, saith the Lord God, surely because my flock became a prey, and my flock became meat to every beast of the field, because there was no shepherd, neither did my shepherds search for my flock, but the shepherds fed themselves, and fed not my flock;

Therefore, O ye shepherds, heard the word of the Lord;

Thus saith the Lord God; Behold, I am against the

shepherds; and I will require my flock at their hand, and cause them to cease from feeding the flock; neither shall the shepherds feed themselves any more; for I will deliver my flock from their mouth, that they may not be meat for them.

For thus saith the Lord God; Behold, I, even I, will both search my sheep, and seek them out.

As a shepherd seeketh out his flock in the day that he is among his sheep that are scattered; so will I seek out my sheep, and will deliver them out of all places where they have been scattered in the cloudy and dark day.

And I will bring them out from the people, and gather them from the countries, and will bring them to their own land, and feed them upon the mountains of Israel by the rivers, and in all the inhabited places of the country.

I will feed them in a good pasture, and upon the high mountains of Israel shall their fold be: there shall they lie in a good fold, and in a fat pasture shall they feed upon the mountains of Israel.

I will feed my flock, and I will cause them to lie down, saith the Lord God.

I will seek that which was lost, and bring again that which was driven away, and will bind up that which was broken, and will strengthen that which was sick: but I will destroy the fat and the strong; I will feed them with judgment.

And as for you, O my flock, thus saith the Lord God; Behold, I judge between cattle and cattle, between the rams and the he goats.

Seemeth it a small thing unto you to have eaten up the good pasture, but ye must tread down with your feet the residue of your pastures? and to have drunk of the deep waters, but ye must foul the residue with your feet?

And as for my flock, they eat that which ye have trodden with your feet; and they drink that which ye have fouled with your feet.

Therefore thus saith the Lord God unto them; Behold, I, even I, will judge between the fat cattle and between the lean cattle.

Because ye have thrust with side and with shoulder, and pushed all the diseased with your horns, till ye have scattered them abroad;

Therefore will I save my flock, and they shall no more be a prey; and I will judge between cattle and cattle.
—*Ezekiel 34:1–22*

But he that knew not, and did commit things worthy of stripes, shall be beaten with few stripes. For unto whomsoever much is given, of him shall be much required: and to whom men have committed much, of him they will ask the more.
—*Luke 12:48*

RIGHTEOUSNESS OVER RITUAL

The prophets of the Old Testament and the Gospels of the New Testament consistently affirm that the best way to observe the law of God is not through ritual or Shibboleth but by demonstrating respect for human concerns in all activities.

SAMUEL

But the Lord said unto Samuel, Look not on his countenance, or on the height of his stature; because I have refused him: for the Lord seeth not as man seeth; for man looketh on the outward appearance, but the Lord looketh on the heart.
—*I Samuel 16:17*

SOLOMON

To do justice and judgment is more acceptable to the Lord than sacrifice.
—*Proverbs 21:3*

ISAIAH

Is it such a fast that I have chosen? a day for a man to afflict his soul? is it to bow down his head as a bulrush, and to spread sackcloth and ashes under him? Wilt thou call this a fast, and an acceptable day to the Lord?

Is not this the fast that I have chosen: to loose the bands of wickedness, to undo the heavy burdens, and to let the oppressed go free, and that ye break every yoke?

Is it not to deal thy bread to the hungry, and that thou bring the poor that are cast out to thy house? when thou seest the naked, that thou cover him; and that thou hide not thyself from thine own flesh?

Then shall thy light break forth as the morning, and thine health shall spring forth speedily: and the righteousness shall go before thee; the glory of the Lord shall be thy reward.
—*Isaiah 58:5–8*

AMOS

I hate, I despise your feast days, and I will not smell in your solemn assemblies.

Though ye offer me burnt offerings and your meat offerings, I will not accept them: neither will I regard the peace offerings of your fat beasts.

Take thou away from me the noise of thy songs; for I will not hear the melody of thy viols.

But let justice run down as waters, and righteousness as a mighty stream.

—Amos 5:21–24

HOSEA

For I desired mercy, and not sacrifice; and the knowledge of God more than burnt offerings.

—Hosea 6:6

JESUS

And, behold, there was a woman which had a spirit of infirmity eighteen years, and was bowed together, and could in no wise lift up herself.

And when Jesus saw her, he called her to him, and said unto her, Woman, thou art loosed from thine infirmity.

And he laid his hands on her: and immediately she was made straight, and glorified God.

And the ruler of the synagogue answered with indignation, because that Jesus had healed on the sabbath day, and said unto the people, There are six days in which men ought to work: in them therefore come and be healed, and not on the sabbath day.

The Lord then answered him, and said, Thou hypocrite, does not each one of you on the sabbath loose his ox or his ass from the stall, and lead him away to watering?

And ought not this woman, being a daughter of Abraham, whom Satan hath bound, lo, these eighteen years, be loosed from this bond on the sabbath day?

And when he had said these things, all his adversaries were ashamed: and all the people rejoiced for all the glorious things that were done by him.

—Luke 13:11–17

And it came to pass, as he went into the house of one of the chief Pharisees to eat bread on the sabbath day, that they watched him.

And, behold, there was a certain man before him which had the dropsy.

And Jesus answering spake unto the lawyers and Pharisees, saying, Is it lawful to heal on the sabbath day?

And they held their peace. And he took him, and healed him, and let him go;

And answered them, saying, Which of you shall have an ass or an ox fallen into a pit, and will not straightaway pull him out on the sabbath day?

And they could not answer him again to these things.
—*Luke 14:1-6*

And it came to pass, that he went through the cornfields on the sabbath day; and his disciples began, as they went, to pluck the ears of corn.

And the Pharisees said unto him, Behold, why do they on the sabbath day that which is not lawful?

And Jesus said unto them, Have ye never read what David did, when he had need, and was ahungered, he, and they that were with him?

How he went into the house of God in the days of Abiathar the high priest, and did eat the showbread, which is not lawful to eat but for the priests, and gave also to them which were with him?

And he said unto them, The sabbath was made for man, and not man for the sabbath:

Therefore the Son of man is Lord also of the sabbath.

And he entered again into the synagogue; and there was a man there which had a withered hand.

And they watched him, whether he would heal him on the sabbath day; that they might accuse him.

And he saith unto the man which had the withered hand, Stand forth.

And he saith unto them, Is it lawful to do good on the sabbath days, or to do evil? to save life, or to kill? But they held their peace.

And when he had looked round about on them with anger, being grieved for the hardness of their hearts, he saith unto the man, Stretch forth thine hand. And he

stretched it out: and his hand was restored whole as the other.
—*Mark 2:23–28, Mark 3:1–5*

Woe unto you, scribes and Pharisees, hypocrites! for ye are like unto whited sepulchres, which indeed appear beautiful outward, but are within full of dead men's bones, and of all uncleanness.

Even so ye also outwardly appear righteous unto men, but within ye are full of hypocrisy and iniquity.
—*Matthew 23:27–28*

PAUL

For he is not a Jew, which is one outwardly; neither is that circumcision, which is outward in the flesh:

But he is a Jew, which is one inwardly; and circumcision is that of the heart, in the spirit, and not in the letter; whose praise is not of men, but of God.
—*Romans 2:28–29*

Circumcision is nothing, and uncircumcision is nothing, but the keeping of the commandments of God.
—*I Corinthians 7:19*

JAMES

What doth it profit; my brethren, though a man say he hath faith, and have not works? can faith save him?

If a brother or sister be naked, and destitute of daily food,

And one of you say unto them, Depart in peace, be ye warmed and filled; notwithstanding ye give them not those things which are needful to the body; what doth it profit?

Even so faith, if it hath not works, is dead, being alone.
—*James 2:14–17*

IMPLEMENTATION: AGITATE, EDUCATE, AND ORGANIZE

It is one thing to espouse values. It is another to affirm them through action. In addition to articulating values like egalitarianism, respect for human dignity, and social justice, the Bible suggests a course of action to insure that those values are realized.

The fundamental importance of implementing Biblical values is emphasized throughout the Old and New Testaments. God repeatedly confirms that He is a god that brings forth justice. When He first reveals himself to Moses He states that He has heard the cries of the Israelite slaves, and He will liberate them personally. Thus the implication is that revolutionary social work is in fact the incarnation of the deity.

Jesus continues this theme at his last feast with his disciples. Following Isaiah, Jesus declares that his mission is to free the captives, and by announcing that the bread and wine shared is his very body and blood, Jesus reaffirms the notion that sharing constitutes the very essence of the way in which divinity manifests itself in earthly form. Presumably followers of Jesus who "do this" in his remembrance are celebrating his concern for humanity and reaffirming their commitment to his principles.

And the Lord said, I have surely seen the affliction of my people which are in Egypt, and have heard their cry by reason of their taskmasters; for I know their sorrows;

And I am come down to deliver them out of the hand of the Egyptians, and to bring them up out of that land unto a good land and a large, unto a land flowing with milk and honey; unto the place of the Canaanites, and the Hittites, and the Amorites, and Perizzites, and the Hivites, and the Jebusites.

Now therefore, behold, the cry of the children of Israel is come unto me: and I have also seen the oppression wherewith the Egyptians oppress them.
—*Exodus 3:7–9*

And God spake unto Moses, and said unto him, I am the Lord:

77

And I appeared unto Abraham, unto Isaac, and unto Jacob, by the name of God Almighty, but by my name Jehovah was I not known to them.

And I have also established my covenant with them, to give them the land of Canaan, the land of their pilgrimage, wherein they were strangers.

And I have also heard the groaning of the children of Israel whom the Egyptians keep in bondage; and I have remembered my covenant.

Wherefore say unto the children of Israel, I am the Lord, and I will bring you out from under the burdens of the Egyptians, and I will rid you out of their bondage, and I will redeem you with a stretched out arm, and with great judgments:

And I will take you to me for a people, and I will be to you a God: and ye shall know that I am the Lord your God, which bringeth you out from under the burdens of the Egyptians.
—*Exodus 6:2–7*

The poor man cried out, and the Lord heard him, and saved him of all his troubles.
—*Psalms 34:6*

The Lord executeth righteousness and judgment for all that are oppressed.
—*Psalms 103:6*

Happy is he that hath the God of Jacob for his help, whose hope is in the Lord his God:

Which made heaven, and earth, the sea, and all that therein is: which keepeth truth for ever:

Which executeth judgment for the oppressed: which giveth food to the hungry. The Lord looseth the prisoners:

The Lord openeth the eyes of the blind: the Lord raiseth them that are bowed down: the Lord loveth the righteous:

The Lord preserveth the strangers; he relieveth the fatherless and widow: but the way of the wicked he turneth upside down.
—*Psalms 146:5–9*

And when the devil had ended all the temptation, he departed from him for a season.

And Jesus returned in the power of the Spirit into Galilee: and there went out a fame of him through all the region round about.

And he taught in their synagogues, being glorified of all.

And he came to Nazareth, where we had been brought up: and, as his custom was, he went into the synagogue on the sabbath day, and stood up for to read.

And there was delivered unto him the book of the prophet Isaiah. And when he had opened the book, he found the place where it was written,

The Spirit of the Lord is upon me, because he hath annointed me to preach the gospel to the poor; he hath sent me to heal the brokenhearted, to preach deliverance to the captives, and recovering of sight to the blind, to set at liberty them that are bruised.

—Luke 4:13–18

And as they did eat, Jesus took bread, and blessed, and brake it, and gave it to them, and said, Take, eat: this is my body.

And he took the cup, and when he had given thanks, he gave it to them: and they all drank of it.

And he said unto them, This is my blood of the new testament, which is shed for many.

—Mark 14:22–24

QUESTION AUTHORITY

Maintaining the individual's responsibility to challenge power with truth is one of the premiere contributions of the Jewish prophets to human civilization. Even King David is held to account by the prophet Nathan. In the New Testament John the Baptist and Jesus upheld this tradition in their disputes with the rulers of their time.

NATHAN CONFRONTS KING DAVID

And it came to pass in an eveningtide, that David arose from off his bed, and walked upon the roof of the king's

house: and from the roof he saw a woman washing herself; and the woman was very beautiful to look upon.

And David sent and inquired after the woman. And one said, Is not this Bathsheba, the daughter of Eliam, the wife of Uriah the Hittite?

And David sent messengers, and took her; and she came in unto him, and he lay with her; for she was purified from her uncleanness: and she returned unto her house.

And the woman conceived, and sent and told David, and said, I am with child. . . .

. . . And it came to pass in the morning, that David wrote a letter to Joab, and sent it by the hand of Uriah.

And he wrote in the letter, saying, Set ye Uriah in the forefront of the hottest battle, and retire ye from him, that he may be smitten, and die.

And it came to pass, when Joab observed the city, that he assigned Uriah unto a place where he knew that valiant men were.

And the men of the city went out, and fought with Joab: and there fell some of the people of the servants of David; and Uriah the Hittite died also.

. . .

And the Lord sent Nathan unto David. And he came unto him, and said unto him, There were two men in one city; the one rich, and the other poor.

The rich man had exceeding many flocks and herds:

But the poor man had nothing, save one little ewe lamb, which he had bought and nourished up: and it grew up together with him, and with his children; it did eat of his own meat, and drank of his own cup, and lay in his bosom, and was unto him as a daughter.

And there came a traveller unto the rich man, and he spared to take of his own flock and of his own herd, to dress for the wayfaring man that was come unto him; but took the poor man's lamb, and dressed it for the man that was come to him.

And David's anger was greatly kindled against the man; and he said to Nathan, As the Lord liveth, the man that hath done this thing shall surely die.

And he shall restore the lamb fourfold, because he did this thing, and because he had no pity.

And Nathan said to David, Thou are the man. Thus saith

81

the Lord God of Israel, I annointed thee king over Israel, and I delivered thee out of the hand of Saul;

And I gave thee thy master's house, and thy master's wives into thy bosom, and gave thee the house of Israel and of Judah; and if that had been too little, I would moreover have given unto thee such and such things.

Wherefore hast thou despised the commandment of the Lord, to do evil in his sight? thou hast killed Uriah the Hittite with the sword, and hast taken his wife to be thy wife, and hast slain him with the sword of the children of Ammon.

Now therefore the sword shall never depart from thine house; because thou hast despised me, and hast taken the wife of Uriah the Hittite to be thy wife.

Thus saith the Lord, Behold, I will raise up evil against thee out of thine own house, and I will take thy wives before thine eyes, and give them unto thy neighbor, and he shall lie with thy wives in the sight of this sun.

For thou didst it secretly; but I will do this thing before all Israel, and before the sun.

And David said unto Nathan, I have sinned against the Lord. And Nathan said unto David, The Lord also hath put away thy sin; thou shalt not die.

—*II Samuel 11:2–5, 14–17; II Samuel 12:1–13*

ELIJAH CONFRONTS KING AHAB

And it came to pass after these things, that Naboth the Jezreelite had a vineyard, which was in Jezreel, hard by the palace of Ahab king of Samaria.

And Ahab spoke unto Naboth, saying, Give me thy vineyard, that I may have it for a garden of herbs, because it is near unto my house; and I will give thee for it a better vineyard than it; or, if it seem good to thee, I will give thee the worth of it in money.

And Naboth said to Ahab, the Lord forbid it me, that I should give the inheritance of my fathers unto thee.

And Ahab came into his house heavy and displeased because of the word which Naboth the Jezreelite had spoken to him: for he had said, I will not give thee the inheritance of my fathers. And he laid him down upon his bed, and turned away his face, and would eat no bread.

But Jezebel his wife came to him, and said unto him, Why is thy spirit so sad, that thou eatest no bread?

And he said unto her, Because I spake unto Naboth the Jezreelite, and said unto him, Give me thy vineyard for money; or else, if it please thee, I will give thee another vineyard for it: and he answered, I will not give thee my vineyard.

And Jezebel his wife said unto him, Dost thou now govern the kingdom of Israel? arise, and eat bread, and let thine heart be merry: I will give thee the vineyard of Naboth the Jezreelite.

So she wrote letters in Ahab's name, and sealed them with his seal, and sent the letters unto the elders and to the nobles that were in his city, dwelling with Naboth.

And she wrote in the letters, saying, Proclaim a fast, and set Naboth on high among the people:

And set two men, sons of Belial, before him, to bear witness against him, saying, Thou didst blaspheme God and the king. And then carry him out, and stone him, that he may die.

And the men of his city, even the elders and the nobles who were the inhabitants of his city, did as Jezebel had sent unto them, and as it was written in the letters which she had sent unto them.

They proclaimed a fast, and set Naboth on high among the people.

And there came in two men, children of Belial, and sat before him: and the men of Belial witnessed against him, even against Naboth, in the presence of the people, saying, Naboth did blaspheme God and the king. Then they carried him forth out of the city, and stoned him with stones, that he died.

Then they sent to Jezebel, saying, Naboth is stoned, and is dead.

And it came to pass, when Jezebel heard that Naboth was stoned, and was dead, that Jezebel said to Ahab, Ahab, take possession of the vineyard of Naboth the Jezreelite which he refused to give thee for money: for Naboth is not alive, but dead.

And it came to pass, when Ahab heard that Naboth was dead, that Ahab rose up to go down to the vineyard of Naboth the Jezreelite, to take possession of it.

And the word of the Lord came to Elijah the Tishbite, saying,

Go Arise, go down to meet Ahab king of Israel, which is in Samaria: behold, he is in the vineyard of Naboth, whither he is gone down to possess it.

And thou shalt speak unto him, saying, Thus saith the Lord, Hast thou killed, and also taken possession? And thou shalt speak unto him, saying, Thus saith the Lord. In the place where dogs licked the blood of Naboth shall dogs lick thy blood, even thine.

And Ahab said to Elijah, Hast thou found me, O mine enemy? And he answered, I have found thee: because thou hast sold thyself to work evil in the sight of the Lord.

Behold, I will bring evil upon thee, and will take away thy posterity, and will cut off from Ahab him that pisseth against the wall, and him that is shut up and left in Israel.

And will make thine house like the house of Jeroboam the son of Nebat, and like the house of Baasha the son of Ahijah, for the provocation wherewith thou hast provoked me to anger, and made Israel to sin.

And of Jezebel also spake the Lord, saying, The dogs shall eat Jezebel by the wall of Jezreel.

—*I Kings 21:1–23*

JEREMIAH CONFRONTS GOVERNOR PASHUR

Then came Jeremiah from Tophet, whither the Lord had sent him to prophesy; and he stood in the court of the Lord's house; and said to all the people,

Thus saith the Lord of hosts, the God of Israel; Behold, I will bring upon this city and upon all her towns all the evil that I have pronounced against it, because they have hardened their necks, that they might not hear my words.

Now Pashur the son of Immer the priest, who was also chief governor in the house of the Lord, heard that Jeremiah prophesied these things.

Then Pashur smote Jeremiah the prophet, and put him in the stocks that were in the high gate of Benjamin, which was by the house of the Lord.

And it came to pass on the morrow, that Pashur brought forth Jeremiah out of the stocks. Then said Jeremiah unto him, The Lord hath not called thy name Pashur, but Magor-missabib.

For thus saith the Lord, Behold, I will make thee a terror to thyself, and to all thy friends: and they shall fall by the sword of their enemies, and thine eyes shall behold it: and I will give all Judah into the hands of the king of Babylon, and he shall carry them captive into Babylon, and shall slay them with the sword.

Moreover, I will deliver all the strength of this city, and all the labours thereof, and the precious things thereof, and all the treasures of the kings of Judah will I give into the hand of their enemies, which shall spoil them, and take them, and carry them to Babylon.

And thou, Pashur, and all that dwell in thine house shall go into captivity: and thou shalt come to Babylon, and there thou shalt die, and shalt be buried there, thou, and all thy friends, to whom thou hast prophesied lies.

—Jeremiah 19:14–15, 20:1–6

JOHN THE BAPTIST CONFRONTS KING HEROD

For Herod himself had sent forth and laid hold upon John, and bound him in prison for Herodias' sake, his brother Philip's wife; for he had married her.

For John had said unto Herod, It is not lawful for thee to have thy brother's wife.

—Mark 6:17–18

JESUS CONFRONTS KING HEROD

The same day there came certain of the Pharisees, saying unto him, Get thee out, and depart hence: for Herod will kill thee.

And Jesus said unto them, Go ye, and tell that fox, Behold, I cast out devils, and I do cures today and tomorrow, and the third day I shall be perfected.
—*Luke 13:31–32*

MASS MEETINGS

Without mass mobilization it is difficult for any value to ever have a positive impact on society. One way accomplished by Jeremiah, Jonah and Jesus is to convene mass meetings.

JEREMIAH

Now it came to pass, when Jeremiah had made an end of speaking all that the Lord had commanded him to speak unto all the people, that the priests and the prophets and all the people took him, saying Thou shalt surely die.

Why hast thou prophesied in the name of the Lord, saying, This house shall be like Shiloh, and this city shall be desolate without an inhabitant? And all the people were gathered against Jeremiah in the house of the Lord.

When the princes of Judah heard these things, then they came up from the king's house unto the house of the Lord, and sat down in the entry of the new gate of the Lord's house.

Then spake the priests and the prophets unto the princes and to all the people, saying, This man is worthy to die; for he hath prophesied against this city, as ye have heard with your ears.

Then spake Jeremiah unto all the princes and to all the people, saying, The Lord sent me to prophesy against this house and against this city all the words that ye have heard.

Therefore now amend your ways and your doings, and obey the voice of the Lord your God; and the Lord will repent him of the evil that he hath pronounced against you.
—*Jeremiah 26:8–13*

And Jesus, when he came out, saw much people, and was moved with compassion toward them, because they were as sheep to not having a shepherd: and he began to teach them many things.

And when the day was now far spent, his disciples came unto him, and said, This is a desert place, and now the time is far passed:

Send them away, that they may go into the country round about, and into the villages, and buy themselves bread: for they have nothing to eat.

He answered and said unto them, Give ye them to eat. And they say unto him, Shall we go and buy two hundred pennyworth of bread, and give them to eat?

He saith unto them, how many loaves have ye? go and see. And when they knew, they say, Five, and two fishes.

And he commanded them to make all sit down by companies upon the green grass.

And they sat down in ranks, by hundreds, and by fifties.

And when he had taken the five loaves and the two fishes, he looked up to heaven, and blessed, and brake the loaves, and gave them to his disciples to set before them; and the two fishes divided he among them all.

And they did eat, and were filled.

And they took up twelve baskets full of the fragments, and of the fishes.

And they that did eat of the loaves were about five thousand men.

—*Mark 6:34–44*

In those days the multitude being very great, and having nothing to eat, Jesus called his disciples unto him, and saith unto them,

I have compassion on the multitude, because they have now been with me three days, and having nothing to eat:

And if I send them away fasting to their own houses, they will faint by the way: for divers of them came from far.

And his disciples answered him, From whence can a man satisfy men with bread here in the wilderness?

And he asked them, How many loaves have ye? And they said, Seven.

And he commanded the people to sit down on the ground: and he took the seven loaves, and gave thanks, and brake, and gave to his disciples to set before them; and they did set them before the people.

And they had a few small fishes: and he blessed, and commanded to set them also before them.

So they did eat, and were filled: and they took up of the broken meat that was left seven baskets.

And they that had eaten were about four thousand: and he sent them away.

—*Mark 8:1–9*

THEATRICAL DEMONSTRATIONS

Another way to dramatize value issues before the public is to engage in political theatre. Two illustrations of this are Jeremiah walking through Jerusalem with a yoke on his neck and Jesus riding through the same city on a donkey surrounded by thousands hailing him with palm branches.

JEREMIAH

In the beginning of the reign of Jehoiakim the son of Josiah king of Judah came this word unto Jeremiah from the Lord, saying,

Thus saith the Lord to me; Make thee bonds and yokes, and put them upon thy neck,

And send them to the king of Edom, and to the king of Moab, and to the king of the Ammonites, and to the king of Tyrus, and to the king of Zidon, by the hand of the messangers which come to Jerusalem unto Zedekiah king of Judah . . .

—Jeremiah 27:1–3

I spake also to Zedekiah king of Judah according to all these words, saying, Bring your necks under the yoke of the king of Babylon, and serve him and his people, and live.

—Jeremiah 27:12

Then Hananiah the prophet took the yoke from off the prophet Jeremiah's neck, and brake it.

And Hananiah spake in the presence of all the people, saying, Thus saith the Lord; Even so will I brake the yoke of Nebuchadnezzar king of Babylon from the neck of all nations within the space of two full years. And the prophet Jeremiah went his way.

Then the word of the Lord came unto Jeremiah the prophet, after that Hananiah the prophet had broken the yoke from off neck of the prophet Jeremiah, saying,

Go and tell Hananiah, saying, Thus saith the Lord; Thou hast broken the yokes of wood, but thou shalt make for them yokes of iron.

For thus saith the Lord of hosts, the God of Israel; I have

put a yoke of iron upon the neck of all these nations, that they may serve Nebuchadnezzar king of Babylon; and they shall serve him: and I have given him the beasts of the field also.

Then said the prophet Jeremiah unto Hananiah the prophet, Hear now, Hananiah; The Lord hath not sent thee; but thou makest this people to trust in a lie.

Therefore thus saith the Lord; Behold, I will cast thee off from the face of the earth: this year thou shalt die, because thou hast taught rebellion against the Lord.

So Hananiah the prophet died the same year in the seventh month.

—Jeremiah 28:10–17

JESUS

And when they drew nigh unto Jerusalem, and were come to Bethphage, unto the mount of Olives, then sent Jesus two disciples,

Saying unto them, Go into the village over against you, and straightaway ye shall find an ass tied, and a colt with her: loose them, and bring them unto me.

And if any man say unto you, ye shall say, The Lord hath need of them; and straightaway he will send them.

All this was done, that it might be fulfilled which was spoken by the prophet, saying,

Tell ye the daughter of Zion, Behold, thy King cometh unto thee, meek, and sitting upon an ass, and a colt the foal of an ass.

And the disciples went, and did as Jesus commanded them,

And brought the ass, and the colt, and put on them their clothes, and they set him thereon.

And a very great multitude spread their garments in the way; others cut down branches from the trees, and strewed them in the way.

And the multitudes that went before, and that followed, cried, Hosanna to the Son of David: Blessed is he that cometh in the name of the Lord; Hosanna in the highest.

And when he was come into Jerusalem, all the city was moved, saying, Who is this?

And the multitude said, This is Jesus the prophet of Nazareth of Galilee.

—Matthew 21:1–11

ORGANIZE TO PERPETUATE THE MOVEMENT

Like Joe Hill who followed him 2000 years later, the last words of Jesus to his disciples were in effect: don't mourn, organize. His disciples vigorously followed his example. St. Peter quickly learned that organizing efforts were to be extended to all people. St. Paul presents some of his tactics in his first letter to the Corinthians.

JESUS DISPATCHES MEN

Then he called his twelve disciples together, and gave them power and authority over all devils, and to cure diseases.

And he sent them to preach the kingdom of God, and to heal the sick.
—*Luke 9:1–2*

93

After these things the Lord appointed another seventy also, and sent them two and two before his face into every city and place, whither he himself would come.

Therefore said he unto them, The harvest truly is great, but the laborers are few: pray ye therefore the Lord of the harvest, that he would send forth laborers into his harvest.
—*Luke 10:1-2*

And Jesus came and spake unto them, saying All power is given unto me in heaven and in earth.

Go ye therefore, and teach all nations, baptizing them in the name of the Father, and of the Son, and of the Holy Ghost.

Teaching them to observe all things whatsoever I have commanded you: and, lo, I am with you always, even unto the end of the world. Amen.
—*Matthew 28:18-20*

PAUL: STRATEGY AND TACTICS

Whereupon, O King Agrippa, [said Paul,] I was not disobedient unto the heavenly vision:

But showed first unto them of Damascus, and at Jerusalem, and throughout all the coasts of Judea, and then to the Gentiles, that they should repent and turn to God, and do works meet for repentance.
—*Acts 26:19-20*

And unto the Jews I became as a Jew, that I might gain the Jews: to them that are under the law, as under the law, that I might gain them that are under the law.

To them that are without law, as without law, (being not without law to God, but under the law to Christ,) that I might gain them that are without law.

To the weak became I as weak, that I might gain the weak: I am made all things to all men, that I might by all means save some.

And this I do for the gospel's sake, that I might be partaker thereof with you.
—*I Corinthians 9:20-23*

ORGANIZE DISRUPTION

Martin Luther King once observed that justice is a precondition for social peace. Injustice constitutes a subtle form of violence which ultimately erupts in social turmoil. Agents of God sometimes act to draw attention to injustice in still complacent societies.

Then judgment shall dwell in the wilderness, and righteousness remain in the fruitful field.

And the work of righteousness shall be peace; and the effect of righteousness quietness and assurance for ever.
—Isaiah 32:16–17

Because thou hast spoiled many nations, all the remnant of the people shall spoil thee; because of men's blood, and for the violence of the land, of the city, and of all that dwell therein.
—Habakkuk 2:8

And it came to pass, as we went to prayer, a certain damsel possessed with a spirit of divination met us, which brought her masters much gain by soothsaying:

The same followed Paul and us, and cried, saying, These men are the servants of the most high God, which show unto us the way of salvation.

And this did she many days. But Paul, being grieved, turned and said to the spirit, I command thee in the name of Jesus Christ to come out of her. And he came out the same hour.

And when her masters saw that the hope of their gains were gone, they caught Paul and Silas, and drew them into the market place unto the rulers.

And brought them to the magistrates, saying, These men, being Jews, do exceedingly trouble our city,

And teach customs, which are not lawful for us to receive, neither to observe, being Romans.

And the multitude rose up together against them: and the magistrates rent off their clothes, and commanded to beat them.

And when they had laid many stripes upon them, they

cast them into prison, charging the jailer to keep them safely:

Who, having received such a charge, thrust them into the inner prison, and made their feet fast in the stocks.

And at midnight Paul and Silas prayed, and sang praises to God: and the prisoners heard them.
—*Acts 16:16–25*

Think not that I am come to send peace on earth: I came not to send peace, but a sword.

For I am come to set a man at variance against his father, and the daughter-in-law against her mother-in-law,

And a man's foes shall be they of his own household.
—*Matthew 10:34–36*

SUSTAINING ORGANIZATION

Organizing, of course, does not occur in a vacuum. The realization of values cannot last if there is not some means by which effective action can be perpetuated. The model of the early Christians can provide us with a number of options for sustaining organization: dues collection, appointment of cadres, delegation of tasks, and so on.

COLLECT MONEY

Now concerning the collection for the saints, as I have given order to the churches of Galatia, even so do ye.

Upon the first day of the week let every one of you lay by him in store, as God hath prospered him, that there be no gatherings when I come.

And when I come, whomsoever ye shall approve by your letters, them will I send to bring your liberality unto Jerusalem.
—*I Corinthians 16:1–3*

DISTRIBUTE RELIEF

If any man or woman that believeth have widows, let them relieve them, and let not the church be charged; that it may relieve them that are widows indeed.

Let the elders that rule well be counted worthy of double honor, especially they who labor in the word and doctrine.

For the scripture saith, Thou shalt not muzzle the ox that treadeth out the corn. And The laborer is worthy of his reward.
—*I Timothy 5:16–18*

SELECT LEADERS

To Titus, mine own son after the common faith: Grace, mercy, and peace, from God the father and the Lord Jesus Christ our Saviour.

For this cause left I thee in Crete, that thou shouldest set in order the things that are wanting, and ordain elders in every city, as I had appointed thee:

If any be blameless, the husband of one wife, having faithful children not accused of riot or unruly.

For a bishop must be blameless, as the steward of God; not selfwilled, not soon angry, not given to wine, no striker, not given to filthy lucre;

But a lover of hospitality, a lover of good men, sober, just, holy, temperate;
—*Titus 1:4–8*

SUPPORT ORGANIZERS

The elder unto the well beloved Gaius, whom I love in the truth.

Beloved, I wish above all things that thou mayest prosper and be in health, even as thy soul prospereth.

For I rejoiced greatly, when the brethren came and testified of the truth that is in thee, even as thou walkest in the truth.

I have no greater joy than to hear that my children walk in truth.

Beloved, thou doest faithfully whatsoever thou doest to the brethren, and to strangers;

Which have borne witness of thy charity before the church: whom if thou bring forward on their journey after a godly sort, thou shalt do well:

Because that for his name's sake they went forth, taking nothing of the Gentiles.

We therefore ought to support such, that we might be fellow helpers to the truth.
—*III John 1:1–8*

SPECIALIZATION

For as we have many members in one body, and all members have not the same office:

So we, being many, are one body in Christ, and every one members one of another.

Having then gifts differing according to the grace that is given to us, whether prophecy, let us prophesy according to the proportion of faith;

Or ministry, let us wait on our ministering: or he that teacheth, on teaching;

Or he that exhorteth, on exhortation: he that giveth, let

99

him do it with simplicity; he that ruleth, with diligence; he that showeth mercy, with cheerfulness.
—*Romans 12:4–8*

Now ye are the body of Christ, and members in particular.

And God hath set some in the church, first apostles, secondarily prophets, thirdly teachers, after that miracles, then gifts of healings, helps, governments, diversities of tongues.

Are all apostles? are all prophets? are all teachers: are all workers of miracles:
Have all the gifts of healing? do all speak with tongues? do all interpret?

But covet earnestly the best gifts: and yet show I unto you a more excellent way.
—*I Corinthians 12:27–31*

CHOOSE AND COMMIT

As there is a time for critique, and a time for organizing, so there is a time for choosing.

And when the morning arose, then the angels hastened Lot, saying, Arise, take thy wife, and thy two daughters, which are here; lest thou be consumed in the iniquity of the city.

And while he lingered, the men laid hold upon his hand, and upon the hand of his wife, and upon the hand of his two daughters; the Lord being merciful unto him: and they brought him forth, and set him without the city. . . .

. . . The sun was risen upon the earth when Lot entered into Zoar.

Then the Lord rained upon Sodom and Gomorrah brimstone and fire from the Lord out of heaven;

And he overthrew those cities, and all the plain, and all the inhabitants of the cities, and that which grew upon the ground.

But his wife looked back from behind him, and she became a pillar of salt.

—*Genesis 19:15–17, 23–26*

No man can serve two masters: for either he will hate the one and love the other; or else he will hold to the one, and despise the other. Ye cannot serve God and mammon.

—*Matthew 6:24*

He that is not with me is against me; and he that gathereth not with me scattereth abroad.

—*Matthew 12:30*

NEGOTIATE

When the choices have been made there comes a time when the representatives of power and privilege must be confronted. Negotiation is an option.

And afterward Moses and Aaron went in, and told Pharaoh, Thus saith the Lord God of Israel, Let my people go, that they may hold a feast unto me in the wilderness.

And Pharaoh said, Who is the Lord, that I should obey his voice to let Israel go? I know not the Lord, neither will I let Israel go.

And they said, The God of the Hebrews hath met with us: let us go, we pray thee, three days' journey into the desert, and sacrifice unto the Lord our God; lest he fall upon us with pestilence, or with the sword.
—*Exodus 5:1–3*

When thou comest nigh unto a city to fight against it, then proclaim peace unto it.

And it shall be, if it make thee answer of peace, and open unto thee, then it shall be, that all the people that is found therein shall be tributaries unto thee, and they shall serve thee.

And if it will make no peace with thee, but will make war against thee, then thou shalt besiege it.
—*Deuteronomy 20:10–12*

THE OPTION TO STRIKE

And the children of Israel journeyed from Rameses to Succoth, about six hundred thousand on foot that were men, beside children.

And a mixed multitude went up also with them; and flock, and herds, even very much cattle.

—*Exodus 12:37–38*

RESORTING TO THE LEGAL SYSTEM

The chief captain commanded Paul to be brought into the castle, and bade that he should be examined by scourging; that he might know wherefore they cried so against him.

And as they bound him with thongs, Paul said unto the centurion that stood by, Is it lawful for you to scourge a man that is a Roman, and not convicted?

When the centurion heard that, he went and told the chief captain, saying, Take heed what thou doest: for this man is a Roman.

Then the chief captain came, and said unto him, Tell me, art thou a Roman? Paul said, Yea.

And the chief captain answered, With a great sum obtained I this freedom. And Paul said, But I was free-born.

Then straightaway they departed from him which should have examined him: and the chief captain also was afraid, after he knew that he was a Roman, and because he had bound him.
—*Acts 22:24–29*

But Festus, willing to do the Jews a pleasure, answered Paul, and said, Wilt thou go up to Jerusalem, and there be judged of these things before me?

Then said Paul, I stand at Caesar's judgment seat, where I ought to be judged: to the Jews I have done no wrong, as thou very well knowest.

For if I be an offender, or have committed anything worthy of death, I refuse not to die; but if there be none of these things whereof these accuse me, no man may deliver me unto them. I appeal unto Caesar.

Then Festus, when he had conferred with the council, answered, Hast thou appealed unto Caesar? unto Caesar shalt thou go.
—*Acts 25:9–12*

CIVIL DISOBEDIENCE

Refusing to obey the laws is an option.

MOSES

Thou shalt not deliver unto his master the servant which is escaped from his master unto thee:

He shall dwell with thee, even among you, in that place which he shall choose in one of thy gates, where it liketh him best: thou shalt not oppress him.
—*Deuteronomy 23:15–16*

PETER

Then went the captain with the officers, and brought them without violence: for they feared the people, lest they should have been stoned.

And when they had brought them, they set them before the council: and the high priest asked them,

Saying, Did not we straitly command you that ye should not teach in this name? and behold, ye have filled Jerusalem with your doctrine, and intend to bring this man's blood upon us.

Then Peter and the other apostles answered and said, We ought to obey God rather than men.
—*Acts 5:26–29*

SELF-DEFENSE THROUGH MUTUAL AID

MUTUALITY: GENERAL

For, brethren, ye have been called unto liberty; only use not liberty for an occasion to the flesh, but by love serve one another.

For all the law is fulfilled in one word, even in this; Thou shalt love thy neighbour as thyself.

But if ye bite and devour one another, take heed that ye be not consumed one of another.
—*Galatians 5:13–15*

Use hospitality one to another without grudging.

As every man hath received the gift, even so minister the same one to another, as good stewards of the manifold grace of God.
—*I Peter 4:9–10*

FIGHTING AND WORKING

And it came to pass, when our enemies heard that it was known unto us, and God had brought their counsel to nought, that we returned all of us to the wall, every one unto his work.

And it came to pass from that time forth, that half of my servants wrought in the work, and the other half of them held both the spears, the shields, and the bows, and the habergeons; and the rulers were behind all the house of Judah.

They which builded on the wall, and they that bare burdens, with those that laded, every one with one of his hands wrought in the work, and with the other hand held a weapon.

For the builders, every one had his sword girded by his side, and so builded. And he that sounded the trumpet was by me.

And I said unto the nobles, and to the rulers, and to the rest of the people, The work is great and large, and we are separated upon the wall, one far from another.

In what place therefore ye hear the sound of the trumpet, resort ye thither unto us: our God shall fight for us.

So we labored in the work: and half of them held the spears from the rising of the morning till the stars appeared.

Likewise at the same time said I unto the people, Let every one with his servant lodge within Jerusalem, that in the night they may be a guard to us, and labor on the day.

So neither I, nor my brethren, nor my servants, nor the men of the guard which followed me, none of us put off our clothes, saving that every one put them off for washing.
—*Nehemiah 4:15–23*

SELF-DEFENSE

Now in the twelfth month, that is, the month Adar, on the thirteenth day of the same, when the king's commandment and his decree drew near to be put in execution, in the day that the enemies of the Jews hopes to have power over them, (though it was turned to the contrary, that the Jews had rule over them that hated them;)

The Jews gathered themselves together in their cities throughout all the provinces of the king Ahasuerus, to lay hand on such as sought their hurt: and no man could withstand them; for the fear of them fell upon all people.
—*Esther 9:1–2*

MUTUAL RELIEF

And when James, Cephas, and John, who seemed to be pillars, perceived the grace that was given unto me, they gave to me and Barnabas the right hands of fellowship; that we should go unto the heathen, and they unto the circumcision.

Only they would that we should remember the poor; the same which I also was forwarded to do.
—*Galatians 2:9–10*

107

SOLIDARITY

In all contexts the importance of solidarity should be manifest.

And the eye cannot say unto the hand, I have no need of thee: nor again the head to the feet, I have no need of you.

Nay, much more these members of the body, which seem to be more feeble, are necessary:

And those members of the body, which we think to be less honorable, upon these we bestow more abundant honor; and our uncomely parts have more abundant comeliness.

For our comely parts have no need: but God hath tempered the body together, having given more abundant honor to that part which lacked:

That there should be no schism in the body; but that the members should have the same care for one another.

And whether one member suffer, all the members suffer with it; or one member be honored, all the members rejoice with it.
—*I Corinthians 12:21–26*

I therefore, the prisoner of the Lord, beseech you that ye walk worthy of the vocation wherewith you are called,

With all lowliness and meekness, with long-suffering, forbearing one another in love;

Endeavoring to keep the unity of the Spirit in the bond of peace.

There is one body, and one Spirit, even as ye are called in one hope of your calling;

One Lord, one faith, one baptism,

One God and Father of all, who is above all, and through all, and in you all.
—*Ephesians 4:1–6*

FLAG DESECRATION

If one makes it a crime to desecrate the flag, one has made a clear statement of one's moral allegiances—one has elevated the flag above any other single object in society, including the Bible, statues of Jesus, etc. The Bible speaks to the issue of trying to contain sacred concerns in material objects.

> **Thou shalt have no other gods before Me.**
> **Thou shalt not make unto thee a graven image, nor any manner of likeness, of anything that is in heaven above, or that is in the earth beneath, or that is in the water below the earth;**
> **Thou shalt not bow down unto them, nor serve them; for I the Lord thy God am a jealous God . . .**
> —*Exodus 20:3–5*

RESORT TO ARMS

In extreme situations the Bible implies that guerrilla war, violence and treason may be appropriate.

GUERRILLA WAR

David therefore departed thence, and escaped to the cave Adullam: and when his brethren and all his father's house heard it, they went down thither to him.

And everyone that was in distress, and everyone that was in debt, and everyone that was discontented, gathered themselves unto him; and he became a captain over them: and there were with him about four hundred men.
—*I Samuel 22:1–2*

TREASON

And David said in his heart, I shall now perish one day by the hand of Saul: there is nothing better for me than that I should speedily escape into the land of the Philistines; and Saul shall despair of me, to seek me any more in any coast of Israel: so shall I escape out of his hand.
—*I Samuel 27:1*

And unto this people thou shalt say, Thus saith the Lord, Behold, I set before you the way of life, and the way of death.

He that abideth in this city shall die by the sword, and by the famine, and by the pestilence: but he that goeth out, and falleth to the Chaldeans that besiege you, he shall live, and his life shall be unto him for a prey.

For I have set my face against this city for evil, and not for good, saith the Lord: it shall be given into the hand of the king of Babylon, and he shall burn it with fire.
—*Jeremiah: 21:8–10*

PURGES

So Jehu slew all that remained of the house of Ahab in Jezreel, and all his great men, and his kinfolks, and his priests, until he left him none remaining.
—*II Kings 10:11*

Then Moses stood in the gate of the camp, and said, Who is on the Lord's side? let him come unto me. And all the sons of Levi gathered themselves together unto him.

And he said unto them, Thus saith the Lord God of Israel, Put every man his sword by his side, and go in and out from gate to gate throughout the camp, and slay every man his brother, and every man his companion, and every man his neighbour.

And the children of Levi did according to the word of Moses: and there fell of the people that day about three thousand men.
—*Exodus 32:26–28*

MAYHEM

And they warred against the Midianites, as the Lord commanded Moses; and they slew all the males. . . .

And Moses said unto them, Have you saved all the women alive? . . . Now therefore kill every male among the little ones, and kill every woman that hath known man by lying with him. But all the women children, that have not known a man by lying with him, keep alive for yourselves.
—*Numbers 31:7, 15, 17–18*

When the Lord thy God shall bring thee into the land wither thou goest to possess it, and hath cast out many nations before thee, the Hittites, and the Girgashites, and the Amorites, and the Canaanites, and the Perizzites, and the Hivites, and the Jebusites, seven nations greater and mightier than thou;

And when the Lord thy God shall deliver them before thee; thou shalt smite them, and utterly destroy them; thou shalt make no covenant with them, nor show mercy unto them.
—*Deuteronomy 7:1–2*

UTOPIA

Whether recourse to violence can ultimately establish a long-standing viable community is open to question. The Bible's promotion of peace and nonviolence accentuates the significance of this issue. In the final analysis what's important are the goals of peace and harmony, and understanding the extent to which these "end" values are created and sustained by the "means" employed to achieve them.

The sort of social ends which the Bible espouses are conveyed in various utopian visions: the social peace expressed through the play of children and the repose of the elderly; the prosperity intimated by John; the eradication of militarism; the universality of artistry; the establishment of justice; the elimination of hostility between humanity and nature and between humanity and humanity.

AN END TO PAIN

And I saw a new heaven and a new earth: for the first heaven and the first earth were passed away; and there was no more sea.

And I John saw the holy city, new Jerusalem, coming down from God out of heaven, prepared as a bride adorned for her husband.

And I heard a great voice out of heaven saying, Behold, the tabernacle of God is with men, and he will dwell with them, and they shall be his people, and God himself shall be with them, and be their God.

And God shall wipe away all tears from their eyes; and there shall be no more death, neither sorrow, nor crying, neither shall there be anymore pain: for the former things are passed away.

And he that sat upon the throne said, Behold, I make all things new. And he said unto me, Write: for these words are true and faithful.

And he said unto me, It is done. I am Alpha and Omega, the beginning and the end. I will give unto him that is athirst of the fountain of the water of life freely.

—*Revelations 21:1–6*

EVERYONE AN ARTIST

And it shall come to pass afterward, that I will pour out my spirit upon all flesh; and your sons and your daughters shall prophesy, your old men shall dream dreams, your young men shall see visions.

And also upon the servants and upon the handmaids in those days will I pour out my spirit.

—*Joel 2:28–29*

SECURITY FOR THE OLD AND THE YOUNG

Thus saith the Lord of hosts; There shall yet old men and old women dwell in the streets of Jerusalem, and every man with his staff in his hand for very age.

And the streets of the city shall be full of boys and girls playing in the streets thereof.

—*Zechariah 8:4–5*

PEACE

And he shall judge among the nations, and shall rebuke many people: and they shall beat their swords into plowshares, and their spears into pruning hooks: nation shall not lift up sword against nation, neither shall they learn war any more.

—*Isaiah 2:4*

LIBERATION

And I will make with them a covenant of peace, and will cause the evil beasts to cease out of the land: and they shall dwell safely in the wilderness, and sleep in the woods.

And I will make them and the places round about my hill a blessing; and I will cause the shower to come down in his season; there shall be showers of blessing.

And the tree of the field shall yield her fruit, and the earth shall yield her increase, and they shall be safe in their land, and shall know that I am the Lord, when I have broken the bands of their yoke, and delivered them out of the hand of those that served themselves of them.

And they shall no more be a prey to the heathen, neither shall the beast of the land devour them; but they shall dwell safely, and none shall make them afraid.

—*Ezekiel 34:25–28*

JUSTICE AND SAFETY

But in the last days it shall come to pass, that the mountain of the house of the Lord shall be established in the top of the mountains, and it shall be exalted above the hills; and people shall flow unto it.

And many nations shall come, and say, Come, and let us go up to the mountain of the Lord, and to the house of the God of Jacob; and he will teach us of his ways, and we will walk in his paths: for the law shall go forth of Zion, and the word of the Lord from Jerusalem.

And he shall judge among many people, and rebuke strong nations afar off; and they shall beat their swords into plowshares, and their spears into pruning hooks: nation shall not lift up a sword against nation, neither shall they learn way any more.

But they shall sit every man under his vine and under his fig tree; and none shall make them afraid: for the mouth of the Lord of hosts hath spoken it.
—*Micah 4:1–4*

JUSTICE AND PEACE

And the spirit of the Lord shall rest upon him, the spirit of wisdom and understanding, the spirit of counsel and might, the spirit of knowledge and of the fear of the Lord;

And shall make him of quick understanding in the fear of the Lord: and he shall not judge after the sight of his eyes, neither reprove after the hearing of his ears:

But with righteousness shall he judge the poor, and reprove with equity for the meek of the earth: and he shall smite the earth with the word of his mouth, and with the breath of his lips shall he slay the wicked.

And righteousness shall be the girdle of his loins, and faithfulness the girdle of his reins.

The wolf also shall dwell with the lamb, and the leopard shall lie down with the kid; and the calf and the young lion and the fatling together; and a little child shall lead them.

And the cow and the bear shall feed; their young one shall lie down together: and the lion shall eat straw like the ox.

And the sucking child shall play on the hole of the asp, and the weaned child shall put his hand on the cockatrice's den.
—*Isaiah 11:2–8*

A NOTE ON SOURCES

Excerpts from the Bible have been taken from the King James version. When the passage does not follow the King James version verbatim, it is because we have adjusted the translation to enhance its comprehensibility.

Certain scholars might object to some of the ways in which we have attributed our sources. It can be disputed whether Moses should be credited with all of the Pentateuch, or David with all of the Psalms. This point is not irrelevant to an anthology which purports to discuss the politics of the Bibile.

Indeed, a whole book might be devoted to this particularized area of "Biblical politics." Much recent Biblical scholarship elaborates on many of the political agendas underlying various primary Bible sources. Freidman illustrates in the recently published *Who Wrote the Bible?* that some basic Biblical texts were written to promote the hegemony of Judah at the expense of Israel, while others were written to promote the interests of one class of Jewish priests over another. The political agendas do not stop there, of course. Everything that is written (and moreover, finally published) has some sort of power considerations underlying it.

However, our concern with Biblical politics has focused on the matter at another level. For this work the politics of the original writings is less interesting than the politics of the final assemblage. For some 2000 years what we know as "the Bible" has been consulted as a moral authority, by groups as diverse as first century mendicants, 10th century European barbarians, 17th century Puritans, and 20th century African-Americans. It is now a part of our culture. The point of *Preach Liberty* is simply to note the extent to which certain fundamentals of our culture ground themselves in basic values such as decency, equality, generosity, and social justice. In this epoch of aggressive greed it is too easy to forget that these values form the foundation of a moral culture. The moment we begin to forget these principles we risk forfeiting not only our heritage but also our humanity.

115

NOTES

Acts 2:42–45
Acts 4:33–35
Acts 5:26–29
Acts 6:1–5
Acts 10:34–35
Acts 16:16–25
Acts 17:4–10
Acts 22:24–29
Acts 25:9–12
Acts 26:19–20
Amos 2:6–7
Amos 4:1–2
Amos 5:6–12
Amos 5:21–24
Amos 6:3–8
Amos 8:4–7
I Corinthians 7:19
I Corinthians 9:20–23
I Corinthians 12:21–26
I Corinthians 12:27–31
I Corinthians 16:1–3
Daniel 4:33
Deuteronomy 2:19–20
Deuteronomy 7:1–2
Deuteronomy 10:17–19
Deuteronomy 15:1–4, 7–11
Deuteronomy 19:1–12
Deuteronomy 20:1–8
Deuteronomy 20:10–12
Deuteronomy 21:10–14
Deuteronomy 23:15–16
Deuteronomy 23:24–25
Deuteronomy 24:5
Deuteronomy 24:11–13
Deuteronomy 24:14–15
Deuteronomy 24:17 [1]
Deuteronomy 24:19–21
Deuteronomy 25:4
Deuteronomy 27:17

Deuteronomy 27:18
Ephesians 4:1–6
Ephesians 4:23–26
Esther 9:1–2
Esther 9:22
Exodus 3:7–9
Exodus 5:1–3
Exodus 6:2–7
Exodus 12:37–38
Exodus 20:3–4
Exodus 21:22–25
Exodus 22:21
Exodus 22:22–23
Exodus 22:25–27
Exodus 23:1
Exodus 23:2
Exodus 23:6
Exodus 23:9
Exodus 23:10–11
Exodus 32:26–28
Exodus 34:21
Ezekiel 13:8–10
Ezekiel 16:48–49
Ezekiel 21:25–27
Ezekiel 22:1–2, 12, 29
Ezekiel 34:1–22
Ezekiel 34:25–29
Judges 4:4–8, 13–16
Galatians 2:9–10
Galatians 3:27
Galatians 5:13–15
Genesis 19:15–17, 23–26
Habakkuk 1:1–4
Hosea 6:6
Hosea 10–23
Isaiah 1:10–17
Isaiah 2:2–4
Isaiah 3:13–15
Isaiah 10:1–2

116